DAVID JASON:

IN HIS ELEMENT

DAVID JASON: IN HIS ELEMENT

DAVID JASON

WITH NIALL EDWORTHY

PHOTOGRAPHS BY

MARK BOURDILLON

GRANADA
MEDIA

First published in Great Britain in 1999
by Granada Media, an imprint of André Deutsch Ltd,
in association with Granada Media Group
76 Dean Street
London
W1V 5HA
www.vci.co.uk

A catalogue record for this book is available from the British Library

ISBN 0 233 99725 3

Design by Design 23
Reprographics by Digicol Link, Bromley, Kent
Printed and bound by Jarrold Book Printing

1 3 5 7 9 10 8 6 4 2

For all the wonderful creatures of the seas

CONTENTS

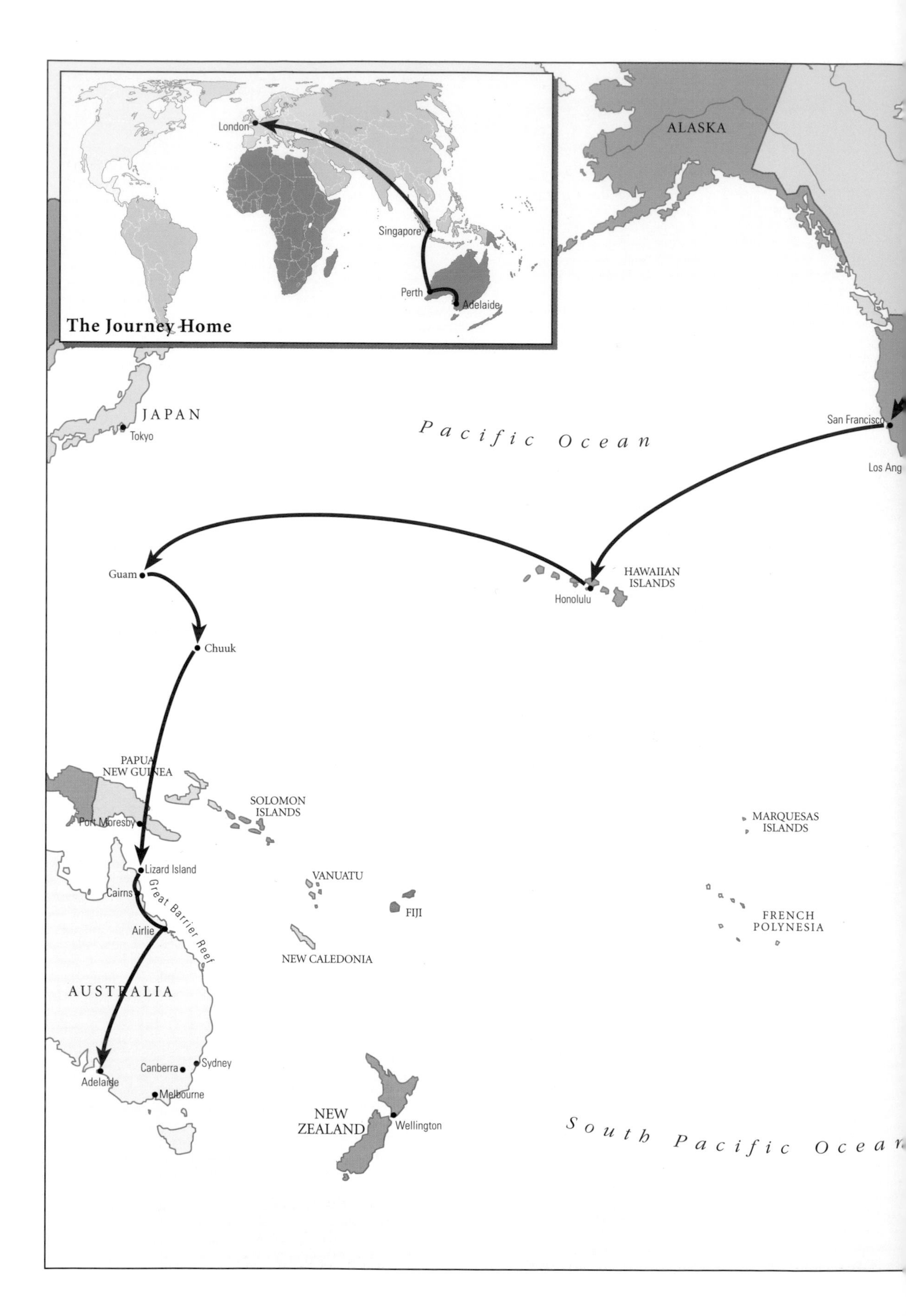
The Journey Home
London
Singapore
Perth
Adelaide
ALASKA
JAPAN
Tokyo
Pacific Ocean
San Francisco
Los Ang
Guam
HAWAIIAN ISLANDS
Honolulu
Chuuk
PAPUA NEW GUINEA
SOLOMON ISLANDS
Port Moresby
MARQUESAS ISLANDS
Lizard Island
Cairns
Great Barrier Reef
VANUATU
FIJI
Airlie
FRENCH POLYNESIA
NEW CALEDONIA
AUSTRALIA
Sydney
Canberra
Adelaide
Melbourne
NEW ZEALAND
Wellington
South Pacific Ocean

GREENLAND
ICELAND
NORWAY
UNITED KINGDOM
IRELAND
London
Paris
FRANCE
SPAIN
PORTUGAL
Madrid
Lisbon
CANADA
Ottawa
Chicago
New York
Washington
UNITED STATES OF AMERICA
North Atlantic Ocean
Rabat
MOROCCO
WESTERN SAHARA
MAURITANIA
MEXICO
BAHAMAS
Mexico City
CUBA
JAMAICA
HAITI
DOMINICAN REPUBLIC
BELIZE
Guatemala
HONDURAS
NICARAGUA
GUATEMALA
Managua
EL SALVADOR
Dakar
THE GAMBIA
SENEGAL
GUINEA-BISSAU
Bamako
MALI
Caracas
TRINIDAD
VENEZUELA
Panama
COSTA RICA
PANAMA
Georgetown
Paramaribo
Bogotá
COLOMBIA
GUYANA
SURINAM
FRENCH GUIANA
GUINEA
Monrovia
SIERRA LEONE
LIBERIA
CÔTE D'IVOIRE
ECUADOR
Quito
PERU
BRAZIL
Lima
La Paz
Brasilia
BOLIVIA
PARAGUAY
Asunción
URUGUAY
Santiago
Buenos Aires
Montevideo
South Atlantic Ocean
ARGENTINA
CHILE
FALKLAND ISLANDS

INTRODUCTION

IT WOULD BE TEMPTING TO CLAIM THAT THE BRIGHT IDEA FOR THESE DIVING programmes had been all mine but that would be very unfair to Major Ned. Like all good ideas, this one seemed so simple and so obvious once it had been aired that I was left wondering why it had not crossed my mind earlier. After all, I have been a diving enthusiast since I was a skinny teenager growing up in north London and through my professional life I have become friendly with people who are constantly seeking to make good television programmes. When Ned Middleton, to give him his proper name, casually suggested that I should consider doing a programme about diving in strange and beautiful locations around the globe, I was on the phone to my friend David Reynolds at Yorkshire Television the very same day.

Major Ned is a very interesting character, a sort of real-life Action Man, who I grew friendly with a few years back. As a former officer in the SAS, the Paras and the Gurkhas who has lived and worked all around the world, he's led a more interesting life than most. He wrote to me out of the blue asking if I would like to sponsor a diving trip to Belize for youngsters on a Duke of Edinburgh course. It sounded kosher and he came across as a very decent character, so I sent him some money for the project. That was the last I heard from him for a few years – apart from a very charming thank-you letter he sent – until he rang and suggested I do a programme called 'Around the World in 80 Dives'.

It was a great title but there was no way we could do 80 dives unless we kissed goodbye to our lives for a couple of years. It probably would have taken about 80 weeks and about 800 flights and, much as I love diving and travelling, I think that might have been a little too much of a good thing. I would probably have returned to England sick of paradise, crying out for overcast skies, traffic jams on the M25 and dinner in the Happy Eater. Or I'd be the only person in the world to be given counselling for Paradise Syndrome – difficulties readjusting to the real world after years of exposure to golden beaches, swaying palms, glorious sunshine, charming locals, exotic cuisine, et cetera, et cetera. Eighteen dives, however, sounded just about perfect although the title 'Around the World in 18 Dives' didn't have the same ring to it somehow.

When we started to discuss the programme seriously we decided that we wanted it to be about more than just diving. We knew that the programme provided us with the perfect chance to show nature, especially underwater nature, in all its glory, but we realized that there was potential to incorporate all sorts of interesting aspects, using diving as the central plank of the programme. Locations are sometimes fascinating in themselves, but often they are nothing without the people who live there and make them interesting. So we decided to 'humanize' the project by introducing weird and wonderful characters with extraordinary stories to tell. (Our producer, Mike Treen, and researcher Judy Kelly would certainly find some weird characters, many of whom were positively certifiable.) Throw in some local history, and we knew we had the ingredients for a very tasty bit of television.

The author in butch mode – realizing that something has eaten the end of his knife

There are plenty of beautiful dive sites around the world, but we wanted ours to be unusual as well. Some, as it turned out, were so unusual – hair-raising even – that I began to wish Major Ned had kept his bright ideas to himself. Such is the nature of television and scheduling that it was something like two years before the production team was assembled and ready for what would become a wonderful adventure and an unforgettable experience.

What we definitely wanted to avoid was just doing a programme about me having a lovely time swanning around various beautiful places, giving off the impression of 'boo sucks to the rest of you'. We wanted to give the viewer value for money – and as you will discover, it's not all glitz and glamour working in television. Far from it being a holiday, when we finally returned to England I was in need of one, as well as two weeks in a funny farm!

MY LOVE AFFAIR WITH DIVING STARTED WHEN I WAS ABOUT 17 AND LIVING AT HOME IN North Finchley in London. Most TV in those days was amazingly dull, but there was one programme which had me glued to the set week after week – *The Underwater World of Hans and Lottie Hass*. It was the first time TV had shown real footage of life under the sea, filmed by this pioneering husband and wife team. As someone whose experience of underwater life was limited to the bottom of my tin bath and the local swimming pool in Summers Lane, I became fascinated by the images of this magical world. It seemed a million miles away from my working-class home in north London and I never thought for a minute that I would ever have the chance to dive myself.

But one day I was browsing through the local paper and saw an advert for the Territorial Army, which had a base nearby in Wood Green. Now joining the TA may not exactly sound like the most exciting prospect for a teenager, but the ad said 'Learn to dive the TA way' and I was intrigued. I had no idea what or who the Territorials were – maybe some paramilitary renegades who'd decided to set up a colony in the twilight zone of the North Circular Road. Anyway, I finally plucked up the courage to go down to the Wood Green baths next to Bertie Bassett's Liquorice Allsorts factory. I walked into reception and began blurting to the man in uniform behind the desk about how I had seen the ad in the paper and how I loved the underwater films of Hans and Lottie Hass and that I didn't want to join the army but wanted to try diving all the same … After about five minutes of me rabbiting on breathlessly the man behind the desk cut me short and said: 'Look, sonny, the pool's next door; I'm the security man for Bertie Bassett's.'

Red-faced and tail between legs, I finally found the right door. There were about half a dozen skinny north London lads all shivering by the side of the pool, arms folded, knees knocking and teeth chattering. We were the latest wave of recruits to the TA – the reserve troops for the British Army, one of the most formidable fighting forces in the world. It was just as well war wasn't declared right then if we were to be the crack troops detailed to save the free world from the might of the Red Army. We made Captain Mainwaring and the old boys from *Dad's Army* look like an elite division from the SAS.

The instructors started us off with a few basic swimming and survival lessons. We seemed to spend a lot of the time either diving into the deep end to retrieve bricks and other objects or tying up our pyjamas and then inflating them into emergency lifejackets – which is not as easy as you might think when you're treading water at the same time. The general idea was that if your boat went down at sea, you could increase your chances of survival by the application of a bit of common sense. I remember that common sense was not the most outstanding personal quality in one of the other recruits on the course who asked the instructor what he should do if he wasn't wearing his pyjamas when the boat started to sink. I think a lot of the TA guys instructing us enjoyed showing up the new boys, but they didn't have to try very hard with that bright spark.

I took my first open-water dive not long afterwards, in an incredibly beautiful coral reef off a tropical island populated by gorgeous women in grass skirts who placed floral garlands around our necks when we arrived and saw that we were given every heavenly comfort we might have wished for … then I woke up. My first outdoor dive took place in a disused brick quarry in Hoddesdon in Hertfordshire. It was December and we had to break the ice to get in. I remember the water was so cold that it actually took my breath away. But I didn't mind in the least. It may not have been exotic but I was incredibly excited about the prospect of my first ever dive. Like everything new when you're growing up, it felt like an amazing adventure. My first dive was – how can I put this? – the second most exciting thing I embarked upon as a boy, if you know what I mean. The most exciting, of course, was being treated to my first ice cream.

Soon after that I made my first dive at sea in the equally exotic surroundings of Swanage on the Dorset coast and it was there that I did most of my diving in the early years. Thinking about it now, I must have been mad. I used to get up at five in the morning at weekends, come rain, sun, snow or hail. I would drive round and pick up a few mates in my rickety old mini-van and then speed off, or rather splutter off in a cloud of exhaust fumes, to Swanage. We got kitted up once we were there and then dived into the freezing English Channel like a bunch of mad penguins in the Antarctic.

More often than not we could see absolutely nothing because the wind and tides stirred up so much sand and silt off the bottom. We may as well have been walking through a desert storm at midnight for all we could see down there. Only when it got dark would we pack up and then set off on the journey home. I remember getting back to London almost unconscious with tiredness. But it was always exhilarating and I loved it.

I dived with the Territorials for two or three years, but as I got more and more involved in the theatre I had to give up my search for underwater adventure because I just didn't have the time. I really missed it, but it was much more important to get my career going. When I took up diving again, about 25 years later, my life had changed completely.

I HAD GONE TO THE CAYMAN ISLANDS FOR A HOLIDAY BECAUSE I WANTED TO GET away from it all, to relax in a place where I would not be recognized and pestered by well-meaning but overly curious Brits. The Caymans are full of Americans and I was just enjoying my anonymity and wandering about the island when I came across a diving shop offering a course whereby you could become a fully qualified diver within a week. All my childhood memories of Hans and Lottie Hass, the Wood Green baths and Swanage came flooding back, and I thought, 'What the hell', and went inside.

As I entered I heard this booming Welsh voice shout: 'Well, bugger me if it's not Del Boy from *Only Fools and Horses*!' My heart sank and I thought, 'Here we go, a bloody loony Brit who's going to stick to me like a barnacle until he's told me his whole life story and got me to sign autographs for every single one of his family of 150 … and their wives … and great-great aunts …' I walked out of the shop but Myfanwy, my lady at the time, told me to go back and sign up for the course, and not be put off by one wally. I returned to discover that the man running the shop was a former British soldier called Ray Williams, who turned out to be an absolute ace of spades. We've been big buddies ever since. It transpired that he was brought up in the same area of south Wales as Myfanwy and my mother. After being injured in the Falklands he left the Army and came to the Caymans to run the dive operation.

When making plans for my TV programme, I said I wouldn't do it without Ray. Apart from being a lovely bloke, he's also a 'Platinum' diver, of which there are only about a hundred in the world. Platinum is the highest level you can reach. The system works a little like credit cards – anyone with a recognized diving qualification carries around a bit of plastic denoting his status in the world. Ray was to be the programme's diving expert, assigned to look after me and make sure YTV's investment returned to the surface alive and well.

You will be hearing a lot more about Ray Williams before the end of this book – not that he will thank me for it!

It was Ray who reawakened my interest in diving during that holiday and when we got back I decided to do the whole course and become what's called a Master Diver – which sounds very grand and swanky but it is not the highest level you can reach (Master Diver is one level below Instructor). Since then I have been lucky enough to have dived in some of the loveliest places in the world – many of them while doing these programmes for YTV – including the Maldives, the Great Barrier Reef, Florida Keys, the Virgin Islands, the Caymans and the South Pacific. Since I took it up again, I have tried to find two or three weeks in the year to go diving. I must admit I have become a bit of a wimp these days and tend to gravitate towards warm seas and sunshine. Swanage loses some of its appeal when it's competing with the Caymans and the Maldives.

It was love at first sight

The lazy diver's way to travel – the underwater scooter

EVERY LONG JOURNEY, THEY SAY, STARTS WITH A SINGLE STEP AND MY FIRST WAS towards my dreaded suitcase to start the wretched process of packing. No matter how many times I have packed and gone round the world on theatre tours or holidays, I never seem to get the packing quite right. Practice certainly hasn't made perfect in my case. As a general rule, I tend to over-pack and end up cursing the unused clothes while I drag my bursting case around for a couple of weeks like a ball and chain.

The problem is that you start packing to cover every eventuality; I could be going to the Sahara, but I would still pack the waterproofs. (You never know, I say to myself, there might just be a freak rainstorm.) I could be going to the Tropics, but there will still be a couple of woolly jerseys in there somewhere. (You never know, there might be a cold snap – stranger things have happened, I reason, and what with this El Niño causing havoc everywhere you can't be too careful these days.) The end result, of course, is that I turn up at my destination feeling like a pack mule and throughout the entire trip I wear a few T-shirts, a pair of shorts and occasionally a pair of trousers in the evening. I could have taken it all in a bit of light hand luggage and made use of the hotel's laundry service.

Maybe one day I will learn, but this time is no different as I prepare for our four-week excursion. You will have some idea of the chaos involved in my packing process if you have read that late Victorian comic masterpiece *Three Men in a Boat* by Jerome K. Jerome, which tells the story of three friends who set off on a boat trip up the Thames. The scene is set for a holiday of multiple mini-disasters when they spend most of the night before departure packing and unpacking their trunks as they keep forgetting whether they have packed their toothbrush or their walking shoes or their first-aid kit. It is a scene which has been repeated many times in my household, although it never seems quite so funny when you are the character at the centre of the comedy.

mares
1

PART ONE – HAWAII

DAY ONE

THE CREW OF 10 (INCLUDING MYSELF) ASSEMBLED AT HEATHROW AIRPORT. THERE were the two cameramen: Jim Hamill, who did the underwater shooting, and Denis Borrow, who did the work on terra firma. Jim actually learned to dive for the programme, so it was going to be an exciting challenge for him to test his professional skills in fresh waters, as it were. Denis is a lovely character, steady as a rock and a very calming influence. The same can be said of Anton Darby, the stage manager, who I have worked with on many projects, including *The Darling Buds of May, A Touch of Frost* and *March in a Windy City,* as well as the first series of *David Jason in His Element*. He is a fantastic second assistant and David Reynolds and I would not think of doing a project without him. He is a consummate professional and has become a good friend. You always want to have someone like Anton or Denis around on a long and tiring project when nerves can occasionally get a little frayed.

Then there was Corky (John) Fountaine, the soundman. You could drag him through a hedge backwards and he would still emerge without a hair out of place – Mr Immaculate might be a better name for him. There was also Mike Treen, our producer, and the aforementioned David Reynolds, the executive producer and director of the programme, both of whom are long-standing work associates as well as good buddies of mine. Then there was Judy, our highly efficient researcher, and a stills photographer called Mark Bourdillon who I had not met before but who turned out to be a great member of the team.

Mike and Judy had done much of the hard work before we had set off by organizing every last detail of the schedule, thus ensuring the expedition did not descend into a logistical nightmare. They had gone out before us on a lightning reconnaissance trip during which they booked flights and hotels and hired cars and boats. They also had to find the best locations to shoot as well as unearth as many interesting local characters as possible. Often when you watch a programme on television you will have no idea of the work that has gone on behind the scenes to produce it. The research and preparation are vital. Then, because everything is pre-booked and often paid for in advance, it is vital that everything runs smoothly because if there is a cock-up or a delay then the whole schedule is thrown out of kilter. Apart from it turning into an administrative catastrophe, it can also create a lot of tension and frustration, which are the last things you want when you are on a long, hard trip.

Oh, and I almost forgot the last but by no means least member of the crew: my favourite Welshman and one of the world's great divers, the inimitable Ray Williams. Ray, true to form, was already making his excuses for things no one had even accused him of. This is one of Ray's many peculiar character traits and I think it must have something to do with his time in the Army. Let me give you an example. While we were in Florida filming part of the first series

So ends another day in paradise

we headed out to find a particular location with Ray sitting in the front of the vehicle doing the navigating. After about an hour it became clear that we were hopelessly lost. 'It isn't my fault, it's the map,' claimed Ray. I quickly identified the problem and turned the map 180 degrees so that it was the right way up. Ray looked momentarily nonplussed before piping up with: 'Oh no, boyo, I was always taught to read maps upside-down – it's what they teach you in the army, you know.' You just can't win with Ray Williams.

It was March and England, of course, was cold, damp, overcast and miserable. As our jumbo jet climbed steeply above London and into the grey clouds headed for Hawaii, I have to admit that I was not overly depressed about the prospect of a couple of weeks in the sun, although of course it is always a wrench to know that you will not be seeing your loved ones for a while. Funnily enough, I usually end up missing the cool and the damp and the greenness of ol' Blighty and by the end of a long trip I am positively looking forward to it. But right now I am happy to leave it trailing in our jumbo-sized slipstream as we set out for the USA on the first leg of a trip that most people would give the right half of their body to be on.

I love the sensation of flying and I suppose it makes it even more enjoyable if you are fortunate enough to find yourself in first class. To look on a map you would think the quickest way to get to San Francisco, our first airport-of-call, would be to head in a straight line in a roughly south-westerly direction. So it surprised me when I looked out of the window and found myself – as I had done on previous transatlantic flights – looking down on the vast snowy expanse of the fantastically inappropriately named Greenland. Covering nearly a million square miles, it is the second biggest island in the world after Australia. It may be cold and bleak and have little by way of nightlife, but from the air it is incredibly beautiful – a great glistening empire of ice as far as the eye can see, crowned by a pink-tinged sky to the north. Staring down at it for what seemed like hours made me realize that there are still huge unspoiled areas of the earth. And long may it remain that way.

During the flight the captain of the 747 invited David Reynolds and myself to the flight deck. I have always been fascinated by flying and have done a bit myself down the years, mainly in gliders. So like a pair of schoolboys invited into the tuck shop, we gleefully crammed ourselves into the tiny cockpit. These flight decks, even on enormous crafts like Jumbos, are so much smaller than you imagine. It always amazes me that these giant flying machines weighing around 388 tons (17 tons of which is just baggage), carrying 426 passengers and 18 crew, are operated from a room not much bigger than the toilet next door to it. There were five of us wedged in there like pickles in a jar with David and I desperately trying not to lean on any of the dozens of levers, switches and gadgets or rows of flashing lights. The captain began to tell us a few stories about some of the flights he had been on.

Once, he said, he received a message from the chief steward that there'd been a complaint from someone travelling in first class. The passenger was fed up with the man sitting next to him who had fallen asleep and slumped on him. The man was so fat that the passenger was unable to shift his great body weight. All attempts to wake him up had failed and the passenger presumed he was drunk. When the steward went down to try and wake him up he realized that the man was dead. At first they asked the passenger whether he would mind if they kept the man there until they arrived at their destination so as to avoid causing a scene amongst the other passengers. Understandably, perhaps, he replied that he hadn't forked out for a first class ticket to spend the entire flight sitting next to a dead body. So the chief engineer on board, not a man to let delicate feelings get in the way of practicalities, took some large black rubbish bags to the first class cabin, wrapped up the corpse and dragged it by the feet down the aisle past the horrified punters in economy, shouting on his way to the rear of the plane, 'Did anybody else have the fish?'

On another occasion, so the story goes, a passenger was discovered dead in the toilet with his trousers around his ankles. They decided to leave him in there, but in order to avoid causing a commotion by having him slumping out in full view of the other passengers, they used plastic handcuffs on his arms and legs to secure him. When they arrived at their destination, they called for the airport authorities to come and take the body away. But when the officials turned up they discovered that during the long flight rigor mortis had set in and the dead body was as stiff as … well, a dead body. As the poor man was still in the sitting position they couldn't carry him out – people might talk – so they had an inspiration. They put him in a wheelchair and covered up his lower half with a blanket before wheeling him through the airport as if he was just an old man having a quick sleep. We told the captain he was having us on, but he swore both stories were absolutely true.

The long flight was painless, almost enjoyable. We had a delicious in-flight

'We said surfboard, Ray.'

meal which actually tasted of food! I always find it amusing when you are handed the menu on some airlines and there is a choice of exotic-sounding dishes, like braised koala bear in a raspberry and chocolate sauce with Himalayan potatoes and carrots Marseillaise, and yet when it comes and you take off the plastic lid it's a cheap TV dinner, made in factory-size kitchens at the airport, tasting of nothing and so hot it takes the roof of your mouth off. But this dish, something involving a chicken, was genuinely delicious. Afterwards I sat back, stretched out my legs and began to wonder what surprises and experiences lay before us. I slowly drifted into a deep sleep with images of beautiful coral reefs and tropical fish swimming around in my mind. When I woke we were hurtling south-west over the great expanse of the North American interior towards the West Coast.

After 10 hours in the friendly skies we touched down in San Francisco, home to the Golden Gate Bridge (actually red), which is one of the longest single-span suspension bridges in the world. It is a beautiful city spread over a cluster of steep hills, halfway down some of the loveliest coastline in the world. The citizens of this cosmopolitan city are famously laid back despite the fact that they live bang on top of the deadly San Andreas Fault. This may sound like another lame excuse offered by Mr Williams, but in fact it is the line where the American and Pacific crusts rub up against each other over a stretch of 600 miles between northern California and the Colorado desert. The two giant plates move past each other at a rate of about one centimetre per year but a sudden underground movement can wreak havoc. At the turn of the century about 500 people were killed and half the city destroyed after a giant tremor hit the area. There have also been major quakes in the last ten years or so, the worst coming in 1989 when bridges, elevated freeways and houses were reduced to rubble.

Unfortunately, we have no time to explore the city because our tight schedule means we will just get whisked off to our hotel for dinner, a night's sleep and breakfast before continuing our odyssey to Hawaii. This is one of the great frustrations of filming abroad. People often say, 'Gosh, how lucky you must be to travel all around the world and see these wonderful places', but the truth is that often the most you see of these exotic locations is the hotel foyer, the inside of the lift and your bedroom, which might just as well be in Neasden.

AT SAN FRANCISCO AIRPORT I'M ABOUT TO GET INTO A LIFT TO TAKE US TO THE HOTEL bus when I hear an English voice shouting, 'Cor! Is that David Jason?' to which I reply, 'No – it was', as the doors close and I shoot up to the next floor. Celebrity is a strange phenomenon with a lot of perks as well as a few downsides. Being recognized in public is certainly a mixed blessing. The trouble is that each person who comes up to introduce themselves has no idea that someone else has done exactly the same thing about five minutes earlier, and someone else five minutes before that and so on ...

When I got my first breaks in 'the business' and people began to recognize me in the street I didn't mind the attention. I must admit that it made me feel good that people appreciated what I did, but after a while it can really start affecting you and can put you in a tricky situation. You want to be as pleasant as possible, but at the same time you want your privacy. That's what I really like

Storm clouds over the Pacific

about coming to the States. Here only the odd British tourist will recognize me and I can generally walk around and go to restaurants like a normal person. It is ironic that most people crave fame, but once they achieve it they crave anonymity. The grass, as the cliché goes, is always greener. But I am eternally grateful to the Great British Public – after all it is their appreciation that has helped me reach where I am today.

Before we can get out of the airport and off to the hotel we have to go through the mind-numbing boredom of standing in endless queues – or 'lines' as they say here – as we are 'processed' like so many cans of beans on a factory conveyor belt. I can't bear this endless faffing and as I stand in line like a good little boy with my EU passport and landing pass, I realize that this is just the first of 18 separate journeys we will be undertaking on this trip: Lord spare us. Perhaps this is what Hell would be like: just endless queues and lots of faceless bureaucrats in brown suits with peaked caps staring at you in an aggressive way. I don't know whether it is just me, but every time I go through Passport Control and Customs these guys have a way of making me feel like I'm some kind of gun-smuggling anarchist who's arrived in their country with the sole purpose of trying to whip up revolutionary fervour and overthrow the government. Or a drug smuggler with several million pounds' worth of dope stuffed in every orifice.

I find it difficult not to start taking the mickey when they start firing their questions about 'purpose of visit' and all the rest, but the trouble is that for those few moments – or hours more like – as you pass through the airport, you are utterly at the mercy of these people. They are in total control and if they decide they don't like you, then they can detain you for hours, turn your bags inside-out, cut open your belongings, empty out the contents of your wash bag. And, of course, the most frightening bureaucratic power of all – the strip and body search, which won't be carried out by Catherine Zeta Jones. Can you think of anything much more humiliating? 'Excuse me, sir, there is just one more place we need to search …' It is always with a sense of enormous relief that I push my trolley past the final Joe 90 character in Customs and back into the free world.

This time is no different as I come face to face with the fat, bald, mean, bored-looking bloke in the cap (I wonder whether it is a requirement of the job to be fat, bald, mean and bored-looking). 'Did you pack the bag yourself, sir?' comes the all-too-familiar inquiry. What kind of a question is that? No matter how many times I am asked it, I still feel a small sense of disbelief at its stupidity. 'No actually, it was packed by some friends of mine in the Baader-Meinhof Gang,' I consider replying. Of course, I say nothing of the sort and stare back at him blankly before announcing with ironic pride, 'Yes, I packed it all by myself.' It is bad enough under normal circumstances, but on this trip the crew will have over 60 (yes, 60) items of luggage and equipment for the officials to investigate. There is supposed to be an express procedure for film crews and other parties moving around large amounts of equipment, but it never seems to make the task any quicker.

The hotel that we've been booked into is pretty near the airport so there won't be any chance of seeing San Francisco properly. It is comfortable enough but much like any other hotel near an airport. I'm staying on English time until we get to Hawaii and, according to my watch, it's 1.30 in the morning which makes it about 6.30 in the evening here. There will be a 6.30 a.m. alarm call before we take our next flight. Our journey has only just begun and already I'm shattered! I'll have a nice refreshing shower before meeting the crew in the bar for a bit of supper and then, trying to fight the jet-lag, get some sleep.

After hours of sitting bolt upright, standing in queues and lugging suitcases all you want to do is lie down and rest your weary bones, but your mind won't let you. Our brains are the most complex and intriguing systems known to science, but they can't seem to work out what's going on when you take them to the other side of the world. They think it's time for breakfast or a beer or a cup of tea; time for anything except sleep. I am told that it is easier to adapt on the return flight from the United States, but that is little comfort now. I can see exactly what will happen: I will suddenly feel desperately tired, go to bed and sink into what appears to be a lovely deep sleep and then about half an hour later I will suddenly wake up, my mind as bright as a light bulb. Then I will lie there for hours admiring the ceiling before finally nodding off again … five minutes before the phone rings and a cheery voice says, 'Good morning, Mr Jason, this is your alarm call.'

DAY TWO

FIVE MINUTES AFTER I'VE NODDED OFF THE BEDSIDE PHONE RINGS AND I HEAR A CHEERY voice say, 'Good morning, Mr Jason, this is your alarm call' and I stagger down to breakfast looking and feeling like a Zombie ...

WE LEAVE SAN FRANCISCO. IT COULD HAVE BEEN SAN FRAN-ANYWHERE FROM WHAT I saw. I'm in the same clothes as yesterday as I was just too tired to unpack anything fresh. Lucky passenger who gets to sit next to me on the flight! And we are on our way to Hawaii – a place described by Mark Twain as 'the loveliest fleet of islands that lies anchored in any ocean' – and I have to confess to feeling a little excited.

I have always wanted to go there as all reports suggest it is a beautiful and fascinating place. (My impressions are based largely on what friends have told me about it and also, of course, on the brilliant 1970s cop programme *Hawaii Five-0* starring Jack Lord, who sadly died at the beginning of 1998.) The whole Hawaiian archipelago stretches 2,000 miles but the cluster of main islands at the southern end extends for 400 miles. From what we could see from the air, the islands look ruggedly mountainous, very lush in some places but barren and volcanic in others. They are all rimmed with beaches, mostly perfect white, although, strangely enough, some of them are volcanically black. And there are the turquoise waters and swaying palm trees, exactly as you are led to expect. The only thing I couldn't see out of the window as we came in to land were the native girls wearing grass skirts and garlands of flowers around their necks and very little else. Maybe they're lying in wait for us at the airport.

Honolulu, the state capital of Hawaii, is on Oahu, by far the most developed and populated of the eight major islands that, along with 124 islets, make up America's fiftieth state. It looks much like any other large US city once you are on the ground. Downtown has the usual quota of high-rise buildings spread out in a grid street pattern and as you drive through the suburbs along the multi-lane freeways you see the endless anonymous malls and burger joints that you find all over the States. It's only when you raise your eyes above street level and see the pockets of cloud nestling into the contours of the mountains that you realize you are actually somewhere pretty special.

We drove straight from the airport to our hotel in Waikiki, which is one of the most famous beach strips in the world. The place immediately struck me as a kind of Marbella for Americans and it is packed to the gunwales with holiday-makers and locals enjoying the dozens of bars, restaurants, tennis complexes, golf courses and parks. The beach stretches as far as I can see and it is full of sunbathers and surfers who have flocked there in their thousands to ride the perfect rollers which crash in off the Pacific.

THE WAIKIKI HOTEL, OVERLOOKING THE BEACH, IS BREATHTAKINGLY BIG AND beautiful. It's set in about 26 acres with dozens of bars and palm trees and looks perfect for a holiday. Unfortunately we are not on holiday; we are working and our schedule demands that we head straight out on our first shoot.

So, after checking in as quickly as possible, we rushed into our rooms and unpacked the equipment as fast as our jet-lagged, disorientated bodies would allow us. As they say in the trade, it was kick, b*****k and scramble. An hour or so later the cameras are rolling.

First we film a scene with a famous local character, Cowboy, a 63-year-old surfer who is as impressive and as brave as any of the muscle-bound youngsters strutting along Waikiki beach ('the surf Nazis' as one of the crew calls them). He is so mad about surfing that he even married his wife while lying on boards out at sea! I don't know about the surfing but one thing is sure – the guy could talk the hind legs off a donkey. I only asked one question and he went on about whatever happened to be passing through his head for about 20 minutes, as if he was trying to break the world record for the longest uninterrupted monologue. He's one of those who opens the fridge door, the light comes on and he does a turn for the audience. You would have thought it was his first conversation with another human being for 20 years.

I am being a bit cruel because he seemed like a genuinely interesting figure, but to be honest, I felt absolutely dreadful during filming. I just wanted to be in bed. I felt totally exhausted after all the travelling and the jet-lag made everything feel slightly spaced out and unreal. I know that it won't take me long to acclimatize, but what is worrying is that my back is starting to play

Where have all the waves gone? Waikiki Beach, Oahu

The Three Degrees. I get a surf lesson from Cowboy and his wife

Me hard at work

up. Bloody marvellous. We are on day one of a four-week shoot where I am going to have to be in tip-top physical and mental condition and my back decides it wants to give me a hard time. Brilliant.

We finish the day's filming having terrible problems with the sound. Poor old Corky, the sound-man, is cursing the radio equipment which went 'tits up' – I think that was his technical expression for the problem – just as the sun was going down. In the end he had to do it with the long-handled boom. (The boom is that thing that looks like a dead cat stuck on a pole that sound-men wave above actors to put them off.) I'm sure it will all be fine, but I feel a bit sorry for him as he had to deal with all these problems on our first day's filming when everybody wanted to get off to a good start.

It makes you realize how delicate the whole filming process is. It just takes one thing to go wrong and the whole shoot is ruined. It could be anything – the guy you are meant to be filming is late, or you get sand in the equipment or the weather intervenes. There are so many potential pitfalls and there are no second chances because the schedules are set in stone and the next day you have to move on to the next stage. That's why feelings often run high on set; you are all aware that there are so many different strands of the process to be drawn together.

That's why I'm a bit worried: the pain in my back has started to spread down my left leg. Imagine if it becomes so painful I cannot dive. It doesn't bear thinking about …

Cool environmentally-friendly traffic cops in Hawaii

A local with a sense of humour. Look carefully – where does the real Supergran begin?

BACK AT THE HOTEL I TOOK THE FLEETING chance to have a lie down and read up on the history of the Hawaiian islands, which I discovered are over two million years old. Oahu is the third largest of the islands, measuring 40 miles by 26. It was formed from two volcanoes which slowly merged into each other over tens of thousands of years. I found it difficult to imagine rivers of hot flowing lava as I looked up at the lush green mountainsides. Apparently, the islands were first settled around the eighth century by Polynesians who journeyed for thousands of miles across the Pacific Ocean in huge canoes with thatched roofs to keep off the blistering sun. They took with them lots of varieties of plants and seeds as well as pigs, dogs and chickens.

About a thousand years later, a chap called Kamehameha (try saying that after a few pina coladas), who was a chief on what is now called Big Island, conquered Oahu. He had been part of a royal party that had welcomed Captain Cook to the islands in the 1770s and it was while on a guided tour of Cook's ship that he came to understand the power of modern weaponry. A few years later, having acquired weapons by trading local goods for them, he set out to conquer the other islands. There followed a bloody civil war with his cousins that went on for two decades at the turn of the nineteenth century. It is difficult to imagine these people viciously butchering each other on what then must have been a paradise more unspoilt and tranquil than it is today. Still, as they say in Yorkshire, there's nowt as queer as folk.

Word spread amongst the world's trading nations that Honolulu had the biggest deep-water harbour in the Pacific and by the middle of the nineteenth century the island was full of rum-swilling, sex-starved sailors from all over the world who made it a key trading centre. (Their modern-day descendants are easy to spot: American businessmen on a jolly from the mainland.) British, Russians, Americans, Portuguese, Japanese, Chinese, Germans and French began to arrive in numbers, creating a very interesting gene pool. By the end of the nineteenth century the indigenous Hawaiians were a minority community on their own islands.

The place did not become an annexed territory of the USA until 1900 and it was not until as late as 1959 that it became a state. Today, the majority of the population (approximately 1.3 million, of which three-quarters live on Oahu) are either Caucasian (of US or European origin) or Japanese, with the

Hawaii's dramatic coastline

rest a mixture of Filipino, Chinese and others. Indigenous Hawaiians make up 12 per cent of the population.

In the twentieth century whaling boats arrived by the dozens while sugar and pineapple plantations were established. The fruit industry formed the backbone of the island's economy until the boom in tourism brought about by cheaper air travel in the 1960s and 1970s (the man from Del Monte had a massive pineapple cannery here until recently, we were reliably informed by our driver).

Even though it was never officially part of the Empire, British influence over the islands was at one point pretty considerable. The first contact with Europe came when Captain Cook arrived in the islands in 1778. Cook later met his death on the islands when he returned a few years afterwards, but I will tell you all the gruesome details of that when we go to visit the scene in a few days. It was another Englishman, Captain George Vancouver, who introduced livestock to the islands a few years after Cook's 'discovery'. (In Canada, they liked Vancouver so much they named an island and a city after him.) After Cook's return to England following his first two voyages around the world, the accounts of his adventures fascinated many traders and explorers, who set off for the Pacific to find these exotic-sounding paradises.

In the nineteenth century Hawaii's monarchs and royal families began to spend a lot of time travelling in Europe, from where they would return with all the latest fashions. King Kamehameha IV was said to be an excellent cricketer and tried to introduce the game to the islands. He even named his son Albert after Queen Victoria's husband. A reminder of British influence can still be seen if you look closely at the Hawaiian flag – up in the left-hand corner there is a miniature Union Jack!

My history lesson continued in the bar where the crew congregated before dinner. We were all feeling a little weary after the rush to get here and finish the first day's filming. But we could relax a bit now because we knew we would be here for a week or so and that we would slowly catch up on some sleep. On first impressions, the young barman did not seem like the kind of guy who would be full of sparkling conversation. He looked like the love child of Beavis and Butthead. He had a goofy face and a stupid laugh, but he turned out to be a lot sharper and better-informed than he looked.

He told us that one of the reasons why you don't see many indigenous-looking folk around is because the native population was severely reduced by diseases, like small pox and venereal infections, brought by European sailors and settlers in the early years of the nineteenth century. One measles epidemic alone killed 10,000 Hawaiians whose isolation from the outside world meant that their immune systems were unable to cope with these alien diseases introduced – as the kid behind the bar delicately put it – 'by you dirty limey sons of ... ' I didn't quite catch the last word.

Judy, our researcher, confirmed Beavis's version of historical events, telling us that the islands even experienced a bubonic plague following the European invasion. About 70 years after Cook and his crew first set foot on the islands the native population had plummeted from about 300,000 to about 70,000. (Later in the evening, my mind began to wander back to the subject of the European impact on native population figures when a couple of members of the crew – who shall remain anonymous – felt emboldened enough by several battleship-sized cocktails to exercise their questionable charms on some unfortunate local girls. With precious little success I should add, but at least it made great sport for the rest of us as we watched their doomed attempt!)

Despite the generally benign climate, the islands have suffered their fair share of natural disasters down the years. Lying just south of the Tropic of Cancer, Hawaii is considered to have the most ideal all-year weather conditions. In the coolest months the average temperature is about 72 degrees Fahrenheit and in the warmest it is 78 degrees, while the average temperature of the sea on Waikiki beach is about 75 degrees. Swimming pools? Who needs 'em? (Incredibly, though, there is frost and snowfall on Hawaii. Winter snows are a common sight on top of some of the mountains, which rise up out of the sea to nearly 14,000 feet, about half the height of Everest. So you can go skiing in the morning and water ski-ing in the afternoon.)

Just after the Second World War and five years after the traumatic Japanese attack on Pearl Harbor, the islands were hit by a tidal wave killing 150 people and destroying hundreds of properties. Another one struck in 1960 killing 57. We are told earthquakes, volcanic eruptions and tidal waves could strike at any time. In 1975 they came all at once. Tropical storms and floods also cause occasional havoc. In 1983 the Kilauea volcano on the Big Island erupted and has been rumbling ever since. Beavis, make mine a double after all ...

DAY THREE

I'm supposed to be diving with Ray Williams to check out the equipment and have an orientation dive. But when I woke up this morning my back was even more painful and I am getting seriously worried about it, as the pain is now shooting down my left leg. I can really do without this. There is enough stress and strain on a shoot as it is, with all the hundreds of thousands of pounds that go into the project, as well as all the time and effort invested by the production team. The programme obviously depends on me being filmed underwater – if I cannot dive, the whole thing is in big trouble.

It would hardly make great television if I'm standing on the boat pointing to the sea and saying to the camera, 'Gosh, I bet there are some pretty interesting things down there.' And then cut to me lying flat on my back on my hotel bed, unable to move, saying, 'Hawaiian ceilings are amongst the most interesting in the world ...'

It seems like I've damaged my lower back and I fear I may have impacted some vertebrae. It might have been on the long flight out here and with 16 more air trips to go I am not feeling overly optimistic about lasting the course. Our scheduled dive is cancelled and David Reynolds and Mike Treen have gone off to have breakfast and discuss a contingency plan. One thing is for sure, we'll need to find a 'back quack' to put me right as soon as possible.

At least I am in comfort though. The room is pretty stunning: I've got a very large double bedroom with an en suite sitting room and double bathroom; there's an enormous television in the bedroom ... and one in the sitting room ... and one in the bathroom! There'd probably be one in the wardrobe if I looked. I know the Americans love their telly but this is ridiculous. Who needs to watch the box when you're doing your teeth?

I sit on the balcony staring out at the bluest of blue seas and the most golden of golden beaches – and hundreds of very Japanese-looking Japanese people. The Japanese here are like the Germans in the Mediterranean. They're the first out on to the beach, laying their towels down to mark out their territory before the rival tribes descend a little later to battle for their own space. About a third of the seven million tourists who visit Hawaii each year are Japanese. No wonder I can never find a sun-lounger.

Along with Bondi beach in Sydney, Waikiki is one of most famous surfing spots in the world. Hawaiian royalty regularly surfed there apparently (an awkward image of Prince Charles riding the crest of a giant curler has just popped into my mind; it doesn't quite work somehow). The beach is two miles long and by mid-morning it is packed with sun worshippers. The sand is beautiful but it was disappointing to hear that most of it is now imported as it is constantly being washed away by the tides. It arrives at night by dumper truck and is raked out to keep it looking constantly fresh and clean.

I decided to take a gentle stroll along the beach, partly for a bit of exercise and partly to stop me brooding about my injury. The first thing that struck me was the waves – or rather the lack of waves. The opening and closing credits of *Hawaii Five-0* had led me to expect waves sixty foot high. Well, at nine

Now that's what I call a view

o'clock in the morning it looks a bit like Bournemouth in the summer. I've seen more waves in my swimming pool. I can see dozens of desperate people out there lying around on their boards, looking for the merest wavette.

The receptionist in the hotel told me later that the waves generally pick up in the morning and that they average about six to eight feet in height. He said that if they get any bigger only the really advanced surfers should try and tackle them. To be perfectly honest, I think I'll be leaving even the six foot ones to the experts. These beach bums and babes make it look so easy as they casually ride the crest of a wave like the guy in the Old Spice advert, before they come strutting out of the water looking like David Hasselhoff in *Baywatch* or Ursula Andress in a Bond movie.

Surfing, though, is actually extremely difficult and you really have to know what you are doing. Getting turned over by a big wave is not something I would recommend and it can be really dangerous if you hit your head on your board or on the sea bed, or take in a lot of water as you get churned over and over. Even if I had the time, I think I would be happy to watch the experts from the comfort of my sun-lounger (if I can find one that is), armed with a nice cold Hawaiian cocktail, thanks very much. I get quite enough thrills and spills from my diving.

The receptionist also told me to be careful when I go wandering along the sea front or on the streets of Waikiki. He said it may look like paradise, but don't be fooled – Hawaii has one of highest crime rates in the USA. There had been a number of assaults and muggings on tourists in the Waikiki area, many carried out by members of the native population alienated by the invasion of foreigners.

The 'strip' of bars and restaurants could be a lot of places in the world, but it's not too tacky. The shopping malls are full of designer boutiques, souvenir shops, and smart art galleries, and there are scores of luxury hotels attracting the more upmarket punters with some serious money to spend. Hawaii sure ain't cheap. The cost of living here is said to be about 35 per cent higher than mainland America, mainly because it costs that much more to import goods by plane and by boat.

Tourism is the biggest business here by a country mile, making up 60 per cent of the local economy and outstripping even the production of tropical fruits, which for many years was the mainstay of the Hawaiian economy (just as mining used to be in areas of northern England and south Wales or just as shipbuilding used to be in Tyneside and the Clyde). Now, if the tourists disappear so does the Hawaiians' income, and that's exactly what happened during the Gulf War in 1990 when mainland Americans, fearful of the impact that the conflict would have on the economy, stayed at home. It was estimated that Hawaii lost about $700 million that year, hotel and restaurant workers went on strike over pay and conditions (I sometimes wonder if they still are), and then the recession hit, making the next few years just as lean. Tourism always suffers in a downturn – it is the first thing people strike out of their financial planning for the year – so places like Hawaii are especially vulnerable to such fluctuations.

I HAD A LOT OF TIME TO PONDER ALL THESE MATTERS AS I HOBBLED ABOUT LIKE AN old man, clutching my back and feeling slightly sorry for myself. The day went slowly and frustratingly by and then it was time for supper. It was good to see Ray 'It wasn't me' Williams. He always brings a smile to my face. We had a good laugh before supper when we made him wear the Jack Lord wig and do a *Hawaii Five-0* sketch. There is something very comic about Ray; he's naturally funny even if he doesn't mean to be. Something is always going wrong (he buys a pair of shoes and when he gets them home he finds they are odd colours, and so on). Today he told us about his latest disaster.

During his orientation dive in the morning he used his look-alike Rolex watch for the first time. He bought it for $399 over the internet from a retailer in America after reading that it was guaranteed to a depth of 300 feet. Today, when he returned to the surface, having been no deeper than 50 feet, he couldn't see the time – the face was completely steamed up with condensation. And this is the man I entrust with my life under water …

After laughing at Ray for about half an hour, we went to an absolutely wonderful local restaurant where you could have Italian, Chinese, American, Japanese, Outer Mongolian, you name it. Virtually every cuisine on earth was available, except English of course! (When have you ever seen an English take-away abroad?) All the food was absolutely top notch and a welcome reminder that there is a hell of a lot more to eating out in Hawaii than just burger bars and pizza joints. While we were umming and ahhing over the food the waiter told us that Hawaii is officially the healthiest state in America. It was a lovely evening and by the time I finally hobbled into bed I felt the most cheerful that I had done all day, although the old backbone was still giving me cause for concern. Anyway, good night (I hope).

DAY FOUR

TODAY HAS BEEN THE BEST DAY SO FAR. AFTER A WONDERFUL TIME FILMING ALL MANNER of marine animals and fish at Sealife Marine Park, I saw the chiropractor ('back-snapper' might be a better way of putting it). He told me that I had only damaged some muscles in my back and not, thank heavens, the vertebrae. It's still very painful but at least I know that with some proper stretching and physiotherapy I will be able to get on with the diving.

We saw some interesting sites on the way to Sealife. Our guide pointed out a tide pool known locally as 'the toilet bowl' because of the way it flushes and refills with every wave. We also saw a stretch of 'Waiahole Ditch' which is a man-made waterway about 25 miles long, including a two-mile tunnel where we are to do some kayaking in a few days' time. It was built at the time of the First World War in what was then the biggest engineering project Hawaii had undertaken. The aim was to boost Hawaii's tropical fruit production by carrying water from the wet windward side of the island to the drier leeward side where the sugar and pineapple plantations were sited.

The filming at Sealife went smoothly as we spent time mingling with and feeding some extraordinary and lovely creatures (no, that does not mean we took some local girls out to lunch). There were sea-lions, Hawaiian monk seals, blind seals, melon-headed whales and something called a wholfin, which is supposed to be a cross between a whale and a dolphin. 'Oh yeah,' I thought, 'pull the other one, it's got sea-lions on the end.' But it's true.

According to our guide at the park the female melon-headed whale, which can grow up to 15 feet, is considered attractive by male dolphins. They go out on a few dates to the local beauty spot at the coral reef, like big fish do in these parts, before she eventually asks him back to hers for a mouthful of plankton and a bit of a cuddle. Nature being nature she offers her honour, he honours her offer (and he's on her and off 'er all night) and a few months later you have your wholfin. They're absolutely charming creatures and it was a wonderful experience to get so close to them.

Monk seals are a highly endangered species, similar to but much larger than an ordinary seal. They are painfully shy which is probably why there doesn't appear to be very many of them about – too embarrassed to show their faces to the people who go around the world making number counts on supposedly rare species. There's probably thousands of them hiding behind a rock at the bottom of the sea.

Hunting and pollution, nature's biggest enemies, have taken their toll as the

A melon-headed whale at Sealife Marine Park, Waimanolo, Oahu

population has dwindled in recent years. Moreover, these aptly named monk seals are so reserved that they tend to shun contact not just with the outside world but also with members of the opposite sex. And you don't have to have an 'O' level in biology to work out why that is another reason their numbers are so low. The ones they've got in captivity at Sealife are absolutely charming and totally trusting because they've been tamed.

The whole wildlife park is brilliantly put together and allows people to interact intimately with the animals, while creating for them a natural environment. I can't imagine how thrilling children must find it because even our fully grown camera crew were exhilarated by the experience. The beautiful location with its huge well-designed pools set in the hillside, overlooking the sea, certainly adds to the experience. While we were there we saw some hump-backed whales just a few hundred yards off the shore spouting great jets of water through their blow-holes. It was lovely to see them in the background to this wonderful park, in the environment where they really belong.

After a highly successful day's filming we came back to the hotel where some of *Hawaii Five-0* was actually filmed. Today it was my turn to do an impersonation of Jack Lord and we had a bit of fun taking off the scenes from the opening titles, which proved to be quite difficult with one and a half

A wholfin, a cross between a whale and a dolphin

The USS Arizona *National Memorial*

cameras and three extras! If it turns out to be any good when we come to edit it, we will put in the programme. What the scene may have lacked by way of research and polish it certainly made up for in spontaneity.

WE LEAVE THIS BEAUTIFUL HOTEL TOMORROW AND HEAD FOR THE ISLAND THAT actually bears the name Hawaii, but for clarity is known as the Big Island, because … you have three guesses. Before we leave for the short trip we are hoping to film at Pearl Harbor, which I am sure will be an emotional and moving experience for us all. The Americans are understandably sensitive about their famous war grave. They won't allow us to film there too much as they don't want the area to be exploited, but I hope we can get enough material to convey the shock of the devastation wreaked upon the US fleet and the terrible loss of life that occurred on that dramatic morning late in 1941.

Before packing and going to bed I saw the osteopath who told me that my back was in a bad state; but what can he suggest, I asked. He said he thought it was a muscular problem caused by sitting so long in the plane on the way over here. He told me that by stretching the muscles in a careful way they should improve slowly. Although I'm feeling a little bit better we run the risk of aggravating the problem, so we'll have to change some of the shooting for the next day or two.

DAY FIVE

Warren Verhoff, of the Pearl Harbor Survivors' Association, gazes across the harbour where he lost many friends and shipmates

WE LEFT THE HOTEL EARLY IN THE MORNING AND SET OFF IN THE TRUCKS TO PEARL Harbor, which is just down the road. (When you are on a Hawaiian island, everything is just down the road.) It turned out to be one of the most moving days of my life. By the end of it I felt totally drained and was virtually speechless.

Most of Pearl Harbor, the principal base for the US Pacific fleet, is off limits to visitors but the war memorial commemorating the day of the attack isn't. The memorial itself is a massive white concrete bridge spanning the breadth of the wreck of the USS *Arizona*, and is a deeply affecting focus for those who come to pay their respects. Below it the ship has remained largely untouched since it was bombed and came to rest with part of its structure still sticking out of the water, still visible today.

It was an extraordinary and haunting feeling to stand at the very place where 1,102 unsuspecting seamen died in just a few moments after the Japanese bombers appeared, literally and metaphorically, out of the blue. The *Arizona* was hit by one of the first of thousands of bombs to be dropped. The forward powder magazines exploded, causing massive damage and as the ship was engulfed in flames it sank rapidly. Most sailors were trapped inside and despite weeks of recovery efforts the bodies of 900 were left inside and the ship was declared an official war grave.

USS ARIZONA BB 39

PEARL HARBOR SURVIVORS ASSOCIATION
CHAPT. 1

In front of the memorial to the 3,434 US servicemen who died at Pearl Harbor

I would have been one year old at the time and totally unaware of those terrible events taking place on the other side of the planet. At the time my mother and father, like thousands of other Europeans, were fighting their own battles. London and other towns were being blitzed and I was living in an Anderson shelter in 26 Lodge Lane, North Finchley, although I cannot remember anything about it, of course. It was later in the war that I can recall hearing the noise of the Luftwaffe, their bombs and the sirens, and I like to think that's the reason why I've never been afraid of thunderstorms. My mother once told me an anecdote about a particularly heavy raid towards the end of the war. Apparently, I asked her what all the terrible noise was outside and, trying not to pass on her own fears to me, she said: 'Don't worry, it's only God moving his furniture about.' Well, he certainly moved it about in Pearl Harbor.

We talked to a number of people who all vividly recalled the day, which for ever after would be known simply as 'Pearl Harbor'. It is strange to think how a place can be transformed from a relatively obscure dot on the map into a major historical event – still known to most people in the world nearly sixty years later – in the space of just a few moments.

One of the first people we came across was a former sailor called Warren Verhoff, who was the chief radio operator on board a communications barge when the attack took place. He had experienced the horrors of that day, but he was one of the lucky ones who somehow escaped with his life. He showed me exactly where the Japanese aircraft came screaming in over the mountains in their hundreds, before swinging around the bay and launching their deadly attack on the US fleet.

We also met Daniel Martinez, a historian who told us everything about the day and the aftermath. It is an incredible story of a few hours that would change the course of twentieth-century history. The attack, which began at 07.53 on Sunday, 7 December 1941, aimed to wipe out the US fleet and thus eliminate America from the war before she had even joined, leaving the way clear for Japanese forces to conquer all of South east Asia, Indonesia and the South Pacific.

In one of the most outrageous manoeuvres in the history of military conflict, six Japanese aircraft carriers of the combined fleet, supported by battleships and back-up craft, had crept silently across the Pacific, somehow eluding American radio operators, before coming to rest about 275 miles north of Hawaii. From there about 360 planes launched a devastating bombing raid. The failure of intelligence services to pick up the movement of the massive naval convoy has given rise to a whole number of conspiracy theories. One of those theories is that Winston Churchill and the British knew about the impending Japanese attack but did not pass on the information in order to ensure that the US would join Britain, then standing virtually alone against the might of the Japanese and the Germans. It is a version of history I do not give much credence to.

The entire Pacific fleet, bar two ships, were in harbour at the time of the attack: 8 battleships, 7 cruisers, 28 destroyers and 5 submarines. The Japanese had deliberately chosen Sunday knowing that the ships would be undermanned. One US army private actually saw the approaching planes on a radar screen but was told to ignore them because a squadron of American bombers was expected at around that time. The Americans were totally unprepared when the first wave of attack by 180 fighters, dive-bombers and torpedo-bombers suddenly burst out of the clear morning sky and unloaded thousands of tons of explosives on what was effectively a massive sitting duck. With the harbour and the surrounding airfields in flames and chaos, a second wave from other carriers arrived an hour later. Most of the damage, though, had been done in the first 30 minutes of the attack.

The dead, the dying and the wounded lay scattered over the whole area, and afterwards the doctors on the island told of how they were unable to treat hundreds of horribly injured victims because they were overwhelmed by the sheer numbers. The casualties, most of them suffering from severe burns and shrapnel wounds, were lined up in row upon row of stretchers on the lawn outside the local hospital, writhing and screaming in pain. The doctors knew that they would be unable to treat let alone save everyone so they were forced to attend only to those with the most realistic chance of survival.

When the attack was over, half of the fleet had been put out of action, although only the unfortunate *Arizona* had been totally and permanently lost. The *Oklahoma* capsized while the *California*, the *Nevada* and the *West Virginia* all sank in shallow water. About a dozen others were also badly damaged although most of the ships could be salvaged – thanks to the shallowness of the harbour – and most of them were restored to active service. Around 200 US navy and air force planes were destroyed, almost all of them on the ground.

Every morning and every night the American flag is raised and lowered at the US Naval Base, Pearl Harbor

A total of 3,434 lives were lost in the biggest military disaster in US history, but if the Japanese plan had been to knock America out of the equation, it backfired horribly. The US government, which had been wavering about entering the hostilities, declared war the very next day – to the relief of the British and her colonial allies. Britain's fleet was being stretched in the Pacific in the defence of its numerous territories. The arrival of the Americans allowed them to divert many of the ships back to the Atlantic and the Mediterranean to face the Germans and Italians. No one was more relieved to see the Americans enter the war than the Australians, who feared, rightly, that Britain's under-strength naval presence in the Far East left them vulnerable to attack and invasion.

We stood in awed silence as the

various guides and survivors recounted the terrible events of those few hours. The *Arizona* memorial is an awesome monument, made all the more moving by the knowledge that below it are the bodies of all those young servicemen who were sleeping or taking breakfast below deck as the first bombs fell with such devastating consequences. Each morning and evening, the flag is raised and lowered by a guard of honour.

Mr Martinez told us that the shrine is regularly visited by a Japanese Zero fighter pilot involved in the raid. Every month he sends flowers from Japan which he asks to be thrown on the top of the *Arizona* in remembrance of the dead.

He also told me of a lady visitor he once saw who just stood stock still, staring out across the harbour for hours. She was there such a long time that eventually he went to ask if she was all right. She said she was from Germany and that she had special reason to thank the Americans for entering the war. She rolled up her sleeve to reveal a tattoo branded on her during her detention in Auschwitz.

We then met three elderly ladies, standing on the memorial, who had come from somewhere in the Midwest. After saving up for years they had finally been able to afford to come to pay their respects to their brother who had been on the *Arizona* that fateful morning.

It is impossible to visit the National Memorial of the *Arizona* and not feel an extremely powerful surge of emotions. I hope that in the film we manage to capture and convey some of it. Daniel Martinez left us with a very touching thought. He said the effects of the attack on Pearl Harbor were like a pebble that had been dropped in the middle of a lake and the ripples still hadn't reached the side. I suppose by that he meant that those still alive whose loved ones died that day are still grieving for the lives that were snuffed out when they had barely begun.

We left Pearl Harbor drained by what we had seen and learned. The crew was very quiet in the trucks travelling back to the hotel and during lunch barely a word was spoken.

LATER IN THE DAY, WITH THESE SOMBRE THOUGHTS STILL LINGERING, WE FLEW TO Big Island, so called because it is twice the size of the other major Hawaiian islands combined. It marks the most southerly point of the United States of America. Talk about going from the sublime to the ridiculous. We checked into a Hilton Hotel called Waikaloa Village, which is probably the most extraordinary place I have ever stayed in. Anyone who saw the American TV series *Fantasy Island* will have some idea of what this place is like. Only the Americans could have created somewhere as over-the-top as this. In the middle of a huge, barren volcanic mountain, they have built something more like a town designed by the 'concepts' people at Disneyland.

After checking in, the receptionist asked us if we would like to be taken to our rooms by boat or train. I jest you not. We agreed that we would like to travel to our rooms by locomotive. We asked if the train had full buffet facilities, but the receptionist didn't seem to find this very funny. With a straight face she said simply, 'No, but we can arrange for room service to deliver you something from the hotel snack menu.' We thanked her and said we would get back to her by sending her a letter once our journey had ended and we

Taking the train to our rooms at the Hilton Hotel, Waikaloa Village

had arrived at our rooms. Again, this went down like a lead balloon. Perhaps to her 'irony' is the nickname she gives to the device she presses her shirts with. Oh, well.

Our train arrived, driven by a man with a uniform like Idi Amin. He's got more scrambled egg on his hat and his shoulders than I've seen on a breakfast hotplate. The train chugs off for about half a mile, down through woodland and along the edge of a lake where lots of boats criss-cross from one side to the other. The captains and crew look like rear admirals with all the decoration and honours sewn on to their caps and shirts. I wonder what they have been honoured for? Politeness beyond the call of duty in the face of extremely rude customers? Risking eternal ridicule by bravely electing to wear the ridiculous outfits in the first place?

When we arrive at our 'station' we find ourselves in front of a huge row of internationally renowned shops and fashion houses from London, Paris, Milan and New York. Glamorous looking shoppers are wandering in and out, laden with bags, as if they were in Bond Street or Fifth Avenue. We take the lift in this giant building called Lagoon Tower and walk for what seems like 15 miles to my room – or more accurately, my luxurious warehouse. We enter the room and I can barely see the other side in the distance. I could house a family of 50 in my bedroom while another 30 could set up home in the bathroom and I would still barely notice that they were there.

The stunning gardens at the Hilton Hotel

I've got a bath that's the size of a swimming pool and a massive walk-in

shower where you could get lost unless you stuck close to the edge. The toilet is in a separate room where the wash-basin is the size of horse's watering trough. You could have a gang-bang in the bed with about four couples (with a bit of luck and if you could find them). There is only one drawback and that is the hundreds of noisy birds on the lake just below my room. Still, given the incredible luxury of the place, I think it would be a little churlish to complain and anyway I could hardly ring reception and say, 'Excuse me, there are some birds annoying me. Could you please have them shot?'

We have been up since six o'clock in the morning and I am bushed – physically, mentally and emotionally. It has been an absolutely extraordinary day and one I will remember for ever. After a brisk six-mile walk around the room to fetch my wash bag I set off in search of the shower with my compass and map, and am thoroughly ready for bed now I've returned. The prospect of sleep has rarely been so attractive. 'A very good naaght to y'all folks', as they say in these parts.

DAY SIX

THIS PLACE IS EVEN MORE WEIRD THAN I FIRST THOUGHT. I CAN'T FIND BREAKFAST. There is a good reason for this: it is about four miles away by train. Normally when you set off for breakfast in a hotel you just stumble bleary-eyed into the lift and then flop into the dining area. It was a strange feeling to be heading for a railway station in order to find our first meal of the day. On the platform Ray and I stared at a map of this giant complex and tried to work out the best way to get to the restaurant – by train or boat? (The airport is closed for redecoration.) Our mind is made up when a train pulls into the station.

We reach our destination but the saga of obtaining breakfast continues. The restaurant is practically empty, but Ray and I still have to queue up and wait behind a sign which says 'Please wait to be seated'. The lady we are hoping will seat us and feed us seems to find us suspicious and spends ages asking us questions and checking our room numbers, scratching her head and umming and ahhing as if she had been asked to explain quantum theory. Who on earth did she think we were? Jail-breakers who decided that a cooked breakfast at a swanky hotel would be their first port-of-call after escaping from captivity? Finally, however, she seemed to accept that we were good citizens and bona fide guests and led us to our tables.

The breakfast is one of those help-yourself affairs. There are great baskets of tropical fruits brimming with pineapple, papaya, avocado, coconut, mango and banana. The hotplates are piled high with steaming mountains of sausages, bacon, and every style of egg imaginable. One hotel breakfast is generally no better or different from another, but I have to say that this one was exceptional. Mind you, after a long train journey and a battle with bureaucracy we had certainly built up an appetite.

I was just beginning to feel relaxed, as if I was on holiday, when we real-

If the train is late, you can always catch a boat to your hotel room

ized we had to dash off for the day's shoot. Whenever we are working we're always a bit rushed and sailing a bit close to the wind. So to make sure we don't mess up the schedule we set off to catch a train to hurtle us back to the main reception – which is in another time zone – where we are going to be picked up by the film truck.

But a small man wanders along the railway line and says, 'Ah am vely solly, but no train – train is bloken down, vely bloken down. You go boat.' So Ray, myself and 10,000 Japanese pour into a flotilla of boats that have been hastily arranged. Ten minutes later, however, we find ourselves back where we started. The rear admiral look-alike at the helm has taken us from A to A on a pretty tour of the lake. We explain we want to go from A to B and eventually we make it there to join the rest of the crew, although we are now 20 minutes behind schedule.

I HAVE BEEN REALLY LOOKING FORWARD TO MY FIRST DIVE. MY BACK HAS IMPROVED a little and I feel ready to take the plunge. Even though I have been diving for years I still get really excited and feel the adrenaline starting to rise before each dive. Part of it is the anticipation of what you might see when you are down there, part of it is the physical sensation of being underwater and part of it is the danger factor.

I love wildlife and have great respect for nature. It is an incredible thrill to swim alongside so many weird-looking and beautiful creatures. On land, you don't get the chance to wander amongst exotic animals – mind you, one does rub shoulders with some strange creatures walking down Oxford Street on a Saturday afternoon. But the exotic animals either run away or they eat you. With marine animals and fish it is possible to enter their world and get to within touching distance of them. Of course, there are dangerous creatures

My first dive of the trip in the freezing waters of Hawaii's underwater caves

I think the action went thataway...

under the sea, like some types of shark, ray or jellyfish, but you are generally safe if you know what you're doing and you're careful. My motto is, 'If you don't know, then don't touch.'

I have always yearned after and relished the feeling of flying or floating in space. I was the original kid who wanted to be a spaceman. I still do in fact. The closest you can get to space on earth, ironically perhaps, is under the sea. I love the sensation of weightlessness and otherworldliness. There is also that lovely sense of escape when you dive into the water and for a short time leave behind all the anxieties and the petty daily worries we have to deal with. It is very relaxing but not in the sense that you can switch off, because when you are underwater you have to be extremely alert. It is a hazardous undertaking and you have the added responsibility of looking out for your diving partners. You are being kept alive only by your equipment and that's it. Any malfunction and you have to know what to do otherwise you are brown bread, as Derek Trotter would say. You have to be cool or you'll find yourself in hot water, so to speak.

On the way we drive to the bleak-looking lava flows on the other side of the island, which is black with volcanic rock. Looking at it, you would have thought that the lava had flowed down the slope and hardened only last week. If it's at all possible for stone to look fresh, then it looks very fresh. It is utterly barren of vegetation and looks like the dark side of the moon. But apparently most of the lava is about 50 years old. I suppose it will take a few more centuries before nature reclaims what was once here. I fear, though, that the entrepreneurs and the building contractors, who have a somewhat more short-sighted and self-interested view of life, will lay down their roots long before the plants have a chance.

We arrive at our dive operation, called 'Jack's', where we meet our guide, Keller, a tall, very American-looking American – if you know what I mean – who announces that he wants to know who the 'talent' is. This didn't sit very well with me and the expression sounds a bit obnoxious to British ears, but it is a very common Americanism for the 'main man'. Keller turned out to be a very charming individual as well as a very good dive operator. Like many Americans, he seemed a little brash at first but in fact is just very friendly and enthusiastic. His dive boat is spacious and comfortable and as soon as we're aboard we all begin to make our 'nests' where each member of the film crew and dive team lays out all his gear. We also stock up on provisions for the day – lots of sandwiches and plenty of cold drinks to counter the dehydration caused by compressed air.

We are soon in the water, exploring these incredible cave-like areas which were formed thousands of years ago when the hot molten lava poured into the steaming sea. An outer 'crust' would form and the lava would run through and create tunnels, both on the land and under the water.

The water was as clear as blue-tinted crystal, but I was surprised how cold it was, considering we're pretty near the Equator, on the same latitude as Bombay and Timbuktu. Even wearing a swim-skin with a polar lining the almost Arctic cold really started to get to us. Keller explained later that Big Island is actually the summit of what is technically the highest mountain in the world. The tallest peak is about 14,000 feet above sea-level but beneath the water it descends for about another 20,000 feet before reaching the ocean floor, thus making it taller than Everest. The incredibly deep water is constantly being churned up and these bone-shudderingly cold drafts rise from the deep. The top layers never get a chance to heat up because the water is in a constant state of flux.

But it was not just the cold that was causing us problems. The current running through these underwater caves is extremely powerful and Jim, the cameraman, was having great difficulty in these conditions. Soon the current began pulling us in all directions and the waves began crashing against the cliff face. We suddenly found ourselves much closer to the cliff than we thought and there was a real danger that we might get swept against the rocks. Meanwhile, our dive boat was also in danger of foundering and Ray decided we had to abort the dive. We set off for the boat, swimming hard against the current and getting colder by the second. I checked my watch: we had been in the water for only about 40 minutes and despite being no deeper than 30 feet our air supplies were getting worryingly low. Ray gave us the signal to surface (he may not be able to find his way off the pavement on land, but you will not find a sharper operator under water). It was with a huge sigh of relief that we were hauled out of the water by the rest of the crew aboard the dive boat.

We sat there with our teeth chattering as our flesh slowly turned from Glasgow blue to white and finally back to a reassuringly pinky hue. Our recovery was aided by a wonderful lunch laid on by Jack's.

We now had a long wait for nightfall when we were due to resume filming. We were beginning to wonder how we might spend the time when Keller suggested we visit the spot where Captain Cook was killed by the natives. It was just a few miles up the coast and so, being the brave sailors that we are, we set off at once and soon arrived at this huge, stunning natural harbour with great towering cliffs behind. Keller told us that there are dozens of deep caves in the cliffs where the islanders used to bury their dead. The bodies of the island's royal family were placed in the biggest caves. No one except the priests was meant to know which cave housed the royal bones. The story goes that the priest would lower a man carrying the latest deceased royal down the cliff to place them in one of the caves. Once this was done, the priest would then cut the rope and the unfortunate 'body-carrier' would plummet to his own death.

In the middle of the bay there is a large monument marking the spot where the man who 'discovered' Hawaii was killed. I got a bit goose-pimply as we

The monument to Captain Cook on the beach where he was killed in 1779

approached the bay, just as Cook and his crew on the *Resolution* must have done 220 years earlier.

Captain James Cook was the greatest navigator and explorer of his age, whose name was known throughout the civilized world. It is no exaggeration to say that he was one of the greatest Englishmen in history. On the first of his three major voyages, he circumnavigated the globe and 'rediscovered' New Zealand, which he painstakingly charted over six months. After that he headed westward into the Tasman Sea and more uncharted territory, where he discovered the eastern coast of Australia and successfully navigated the Great Barrier Reef, which even today is regarded as one of the most difficult navigational challenges in the world.

In order to find a way through the great maze of coral Cook would often get out of his boat, climb the highest hill overlooking the sea and use his telescope to plot the route. We are going to the Great Barrier Reef in a couple of weeks and it will be fascinating to see for ourselves the difficulties that faced Cook and his crew all those years ago.

Nowadays it is thrilling enough to come half-way round the globe and visit these places. Unlike Cook and his generation we can set off from home knowing for a fact that our destinations exist and that we'll almost definitely be coming back. And, thanks to television and books, we know a fair amount about the history and culture of these foreign places. I can't imagine what it must have been like for Cook and his crew members when they came across these strange lands after months and months at sea in a wooden ship, as far away from home as it is possible to be. Voyaging into the unknown as they did, it must have been the equivalent of space travel in the 1960s. You begin to understand the great sense of joy, relief and excitement these adventurers would have felt when they heard the lad in the crow's nest shout 'Land ahoy!'

Cook set off on his second voyage in 1772 in search of the so-called Terra Australis, a great continent which many believed existed at the most southerly point of the globe. He returned to England three years later to report, accurately as it turned out, that if there was any land mass there then it was completely covered in ice. He had circumnavigated Antarctica.

For his third and final voyage in 1776 he set out with two ships, the *Resolution* and the *Discovery*, to discover if there was a north-west passage around Canada and Alaska or a north-east one around Siberia linking the Pacific and the Atlantic. After finding no way through the great masses of land and ice he encountered, Cook decided to head south to winter at Hawaii (having been the first Europeans to visit the islands the year before), exploring the north-west coast of Canada and America on the way.

When they returned and sailed into Kealakekua Bay, which we visited today, the natives were not just friendly, they treated Cook with almost embarrassing reverence because they believed him to be the reincarnation of their gods. They showered him with gifts and honours and Cook, ever the diplomatic Englishman, returned their honours with gifts of his own. After a week of hospitality Cook set off on a brief trip to chart neighbouring islands, but the *Resolution* damaged a mast in a severe gale and so they returned to the bay to repair it.

This time relations between the seamen and the natives went rapidly downhill when some of the latter stole property from the visitors, including one of the ship's smaller boats, used to carry men to and from the shore. After a number of quarrels Cook decided to take the island's chief hostage until the items had been returned. But as they tried to take the chief back to the ship fighting broke out between Cook's landing party and the hundreds of natives amassed on the shore. In the fracas Cook was stabbed to death and then dragged ashore and butchered. Local legend has it that the natives boiled Cook's dismembered body and then ate him because they thought that by doing so they would assume some of his greatness. (The last bit should be taken with a pinch of salt – the last bit of the story, not Captain Cook, that is.)

From our boat we could see the monument marking the place where Cook was supposedly slain. It is in the middle of a small square on the shoreline, accessible only by sea, and this little plot of land has been declared English territory. 'There is a corner of a foreign field that will be for ever England ...'

After our fascinating diversion, we sailed back down the beautiful coastline to our designated area where we were to drop anchor and wait for the sun to go down. The aim of the shoot was to film me swimming with the giant manta rays. I was reminded of the differences between the British and American senses of humour when I joked with Keller that I would question his competence on film if the rays failed to show up. It was only a light-hearted bit of banter but he took this threat to heart and, looking at me with a very anxious expression, he said he would do his best to 'deliver the goods'.

When darkness descended Keller turned some powerful lights on to the water. The light attracts plankton – the staple diet of many large marine creatures – which in turn attracts the manta rays. The arrival of dozens of other divers at this well-known site was bad news all round. I don't want to sound like a kill-joy but when other divers turn up my heart always sinks. One of the great attractions of diving is the feeling of being in a world of your own, far away from the bustle of human society. You feel at one with nature and the elements. But that sense of tranquillity is shattered when other boats pull up alongside and half the world seems to take the plunge. It feels as if you are in a public swimming pool – albeit a very big and very beautiful one.

Keller decided to dive in ahead of us to check if any of the rays had appeared and told us to kit up. He seemed to be underwater for an eternity when he suddenly appeared out of the inky blackness shouting, 'They're here! They're here! Get your cameras and get in!' Jim, the camera operator, gets in first in case the rays don't stick around too long. After waiting around all day I felt a great surge of excitement, jumped into my wet-suit and plunged overboard. We followed the luminescent trail left by Keller for a while and then, quite suddenly, right before us was this absolutely huge manta ray, flying at speed through the water. It must have been a good two metres across and it swum round and round in front of the lights, flapping its giant 'wings'. It appeared to be ignoring us and the other divers who had quickly appeared on the scene, but it seemed to be attracted by the light or possibly all the plankton that had been illuminated.

Most people were taking still photographs, but I knew I had a job to do to try and capture this magnificent creature on film and get as close to it as I could. It's common diving knowledge that you don't try and touch the ray, or most other sea creatures for that matter. Some of them obviously do not want to be touched and might bite or sting you, but there is another reason. Many

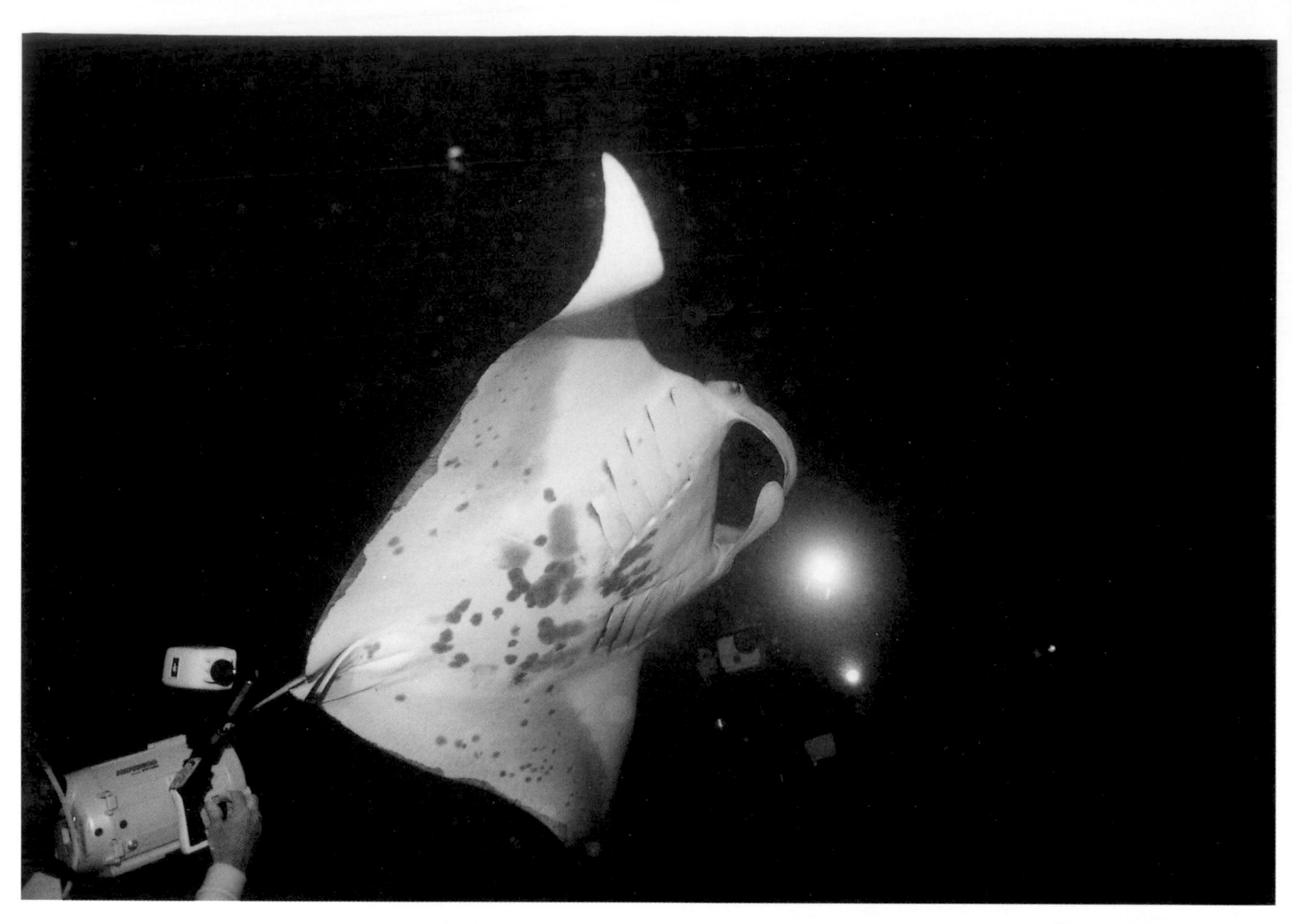

Dancing with the giant manta rays. Attracted by the light, they swoop out of the darkness

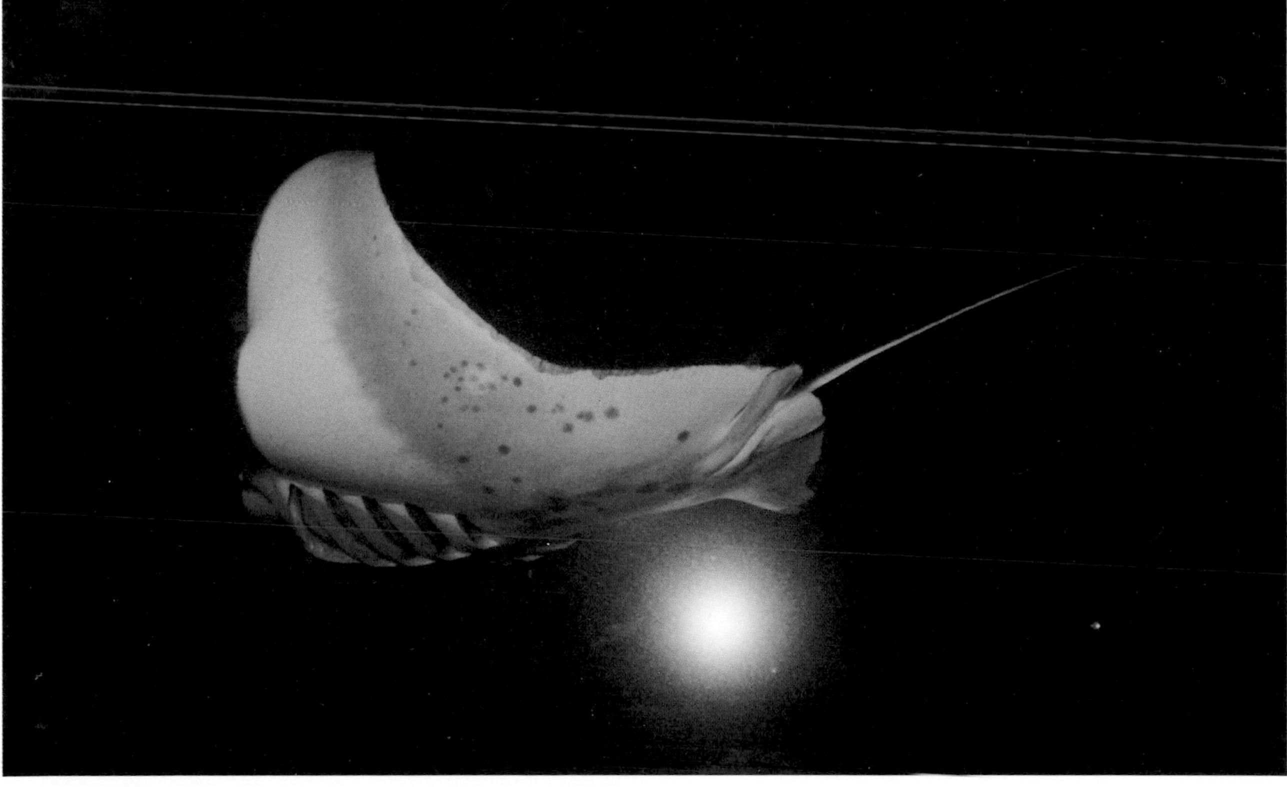

of these creatures are coated with a fine mucus which protects them from infection, and if you touch them sometimes it will rub off and thus expose them to illness.

A light shone in front of me and suddenly one of them swept out of the darkness and 'flew' right over my head, with its mouth wide open – the mouth must have been a good metre across and almost a metre high and I could see right into it. Even though it was heading straight for me, I didn't feel any sense of danger, just an incredible awe at the beauty of these bizarre creatures. At the very last moment, when it was a matter of inches away from me, it swerved, following my torchlight up towards the surface where it did a back somersault and came round again.

It was as if it knew that I desperately wanted to be near it. I honestly had this sensation that it was trying to oblige us as it kept coming back and forth to me time and time again. It got so close that I could see right into its eyes, which at times were only inches away from me as it performed its marine ballet for us. It was one of the most stunning, moving and romantic moments that I had experienced for many a year in the depths of the ocean. What a display. I really hope we've managed to capture the beauty and exhilaration of it on film. I was snapped out of my trance by the alarm on my computer telling me my air was low and with the greatest reluctance I left this magnificent spectacle.

We returned to shore and headed out for a drink and a meal at the end of

Time out for lunch while the crew discuss the next shoot

another incredible day. We found a lovely local sea-front bar where we had a few beers and some delicious seafood and nattered for hours about the day's experiences. In the afterglow of the excitement I hadn't realized how tired I was. On returning to my hotel room I collapsed on my bed and, within seconds of putting my head on the pillow, I went out like a light.

DAY SEVEN

I AM WOKEN OUT OF A VERY DEEP SLEEP BY AN EARLY MORNING ALARM CALL. TODAY we're off to Big Island's famous ditches – canals to you and me – which were constructed to irrigate the sugar plantations on the other side of the island. The plan is to meet up with a guy called Rodney (now where have I heard that name before?). Rodney is the man in charge of operating the ditches and will lead us on a kayak ride through this stunning landscape. These ditches, which are just wide enough to take a small boat, stretch for about 25 miles around the island, dropping only about 72 feet as they twist their way around the mountains.

Flushed with excitement while kayaking down Kohala mountain

SUPER SOFT

After meeting Rodders we piled into one little van to get to the start of the ride. It was like the Black Hole of Hawaii in there. There must have been twenty of us, all sitting on each other's laps and heads with arms and legs sticking out in every direction as we set off, with the kayaks on a trailer at the back, for what we thought would be a short journey around the corner. The 'short journey' turned out to be an hour-long odyssey as we bumped and crawled our way miles up the mountainside, bouncing around in our vehicle like ping-pong balls in a tombola for the big draw. The only comfort on this mini-endurance test was the view out of the window.

The higher we climbed the more majestic became the panorama of this breathtaking land- and sea-scape. We were half-way up the highest mountain in Hawaii and below us in every direction lay miles of green fields and palm trees. Beyond that there is nothing but the deep blue sea stretching into the distance, where it merges seamlessly into the cloudless blue sky.

After finally arriving at our start point we immediately went to work on the filming. It was a bit of a stop-start, laborious process as we canoed for a bit, then moved the camera a little further along the canal and so on until we got a decent sequence of film together. Communication was the most difficult part as we tried to co-ordinate where, amongst all the thick jungle vegetation and winding tunnels, we would meet up for the next sequence.

The shoot descended into a very amusing farce at one point when I was lying in the back of this little boat with my feet poking out the end. Ray Williams, who's slightly ahead of us in another kayak, suddenly starts laughing uncontrollably like a madman being dragged off to the asylum. He howls so much that he falls out of his kayak into the drink.

The source of his mirth, it turned out, was my shoes. When I look down I see that I have on two different style shoes, one of which has a red sole and the other a white one (more observant viewers of the programme will pick up this little curiosity). Ray thought this was probably the funniest thing since he'd been told the one about the chicken who crossed the road. The joke, however, was on him as he was supposed to be in charge of wardrobe and make-up, which didn't go down very well with David Reynolds!

In the end we got all the shots we needed for a good few scenes and the kayaking was great fun (even if we got a little wet) but would have been even better if we hadn't been stopping and starting.

Travelling down this great water conduit you appreciate just how it is a remarkable piece of engineering. As you descend the mountainside with its stunning views you pass through wild jungles and waterfalls, over deep gorges and chasms with raging torrents of water, and through long, dark tunnels hewn out of the mountainside by hundreds of navvies. Rodney and his very likeable and efficient crew also helped make it an unforgettable experience.

We had a good get-together in the hotel bar this evening although one member of the crew went to bed in something less than a wonderful mood. When we arrived in the bar area we saw our friend, who shall remain anonymous (he has suffered enough and, no, it's not the scuba guru this time), in heavy conversation with a rather gorgeous looking local. He made it quite obvious that we weren't to be invited to join their company. When Casanova went to the toilet I thought it only fair to inform this charming young lady that the gentlemen she was talking to was, in fact, a homosexual and that she

The scuba guru humbling himself before the 'Super Soft God of Wrong Shoes'

would therefore be perfectly safe in his company.

An hour or so later the pair left the bar together only for him to return shortly after, looking a little miffed to say the least. It transpired that he had escorted her to her room where she thanked him for his chivalry, saying she knew she would be safe after his friends had told her that he was gay. She kissed him on the cheek and shut the door in his face. He still doesn't know it was me who spilt the beans, and I'm still not telling him!

DAY EIGHT

I HAD THOUGHT THE BUBONIC PLAGUE WAS MEANT TO HAVE DIED OUT LAST CENTURY. I woke up feeling absolutely dreadful, suffering from the most extreme flu symptoms you can imagine. Aches, pains, sore throat, streaming eyes and nose and overwhelming fatigue. I could barely get out of bed. As it turns out, I am not the only one feeling like death warmed up. Ray and Jim have also gone down like felled trees. We try to do some filming, but there's no way we can carry on in this state – apart from anything else, I can hardly go in front of the camera looking and sounding like an advert for Night Nurse. When I began to feel even worse I was driven straight back to the hotel.

Ray tries to remember where he left his hat

Once again, we had to mess around the schedule as our best-laid plans were wrecked by fickle Mother Nature. Still, in a funny kind of way, I am glad it is not just me feeling poorly. According to the doctor who came to see us in our rooms, we are all suffering from 'Hawaiian flu', a common complaint affecting visitors to the islands. They think it is caused by bacteria that lives in the volcanic ash to which natives have become immune. Needless to say, there isn't too much volcanic ash down my way back home, but I think we are especially vulnerable because we are all a little run down from the travelling and the early starts.

I can't believe that yet again the whole project is under threat because of ill health. In my gloomy thoughts I am even imagining that maybe we'll all be going home early and the programme will have to be shelved. It is difficult to feel positive and upbeat when you are ill at the best of times, but when you have something really important to do it is even worse. The doctor prescribed me pills the size of ostrich eggs and told me that even though the symptoms feel fairly severe I will almost certainly feel pretty much back to normal tomorrow. He said that he had seen hundreds of cases of

'Hawaiian flu' and that only in very rare cases did it last longer than 24 hours.

Luckily the rest of the day had been designated as the one day off in the entire trip. I say 'luckily' because it means that the schedule will not be disrupted too much, but it is annoying because I really wanted to be able to get out and explore this place – on my own terms. I had planned to spend some of our day off visiting the island's active volcano, but there'll be no time for that now. We are prisoners of our schedule. Our work is obviously paramount and if we manage to snatch the odd moment of relaxation then that is just a bonus. We have to be professional – that's what we get paid money for.

As it is, I spend the day lying around in my hotel room staring blankly out of the window. From my sick bed I can see glorious sunshine, palm trees, waves breaking on the sandy beaches and lots of happy people having a whale of time. Below my balcony is a huge pool with lots of dolphins in it and on the hotel's own television channel I see there is an in-house lottery offering guests the chance of winning an opportunity to swim with them. They are wonderful creatures and I couldn't help thinking that I'd prefer to be looking at them in the wild rather than in 'captivity' – albeit pretty luxurious captivity. Perhaps it was being cooped up myself, unable to go and enjoy the world beyond, that made me feel especially sympathetic towards the dolphins.

But when I am lying around feeling a bit down in the mouth like I am today, I keep reminding myself how lucky I am to be here in the first place. I worked as an electrician before I made a breakthrough into the professional theatre and I suppose I could be an ageing sparky somewhere back in north London now. I am a lad from a working-class family in North Finchley who hasn't done too bad for himself. That's what I keep telling myself. I am always aware of my roots when I come to places like this and I like to remind myself of how fortunate I am.

Then these thoughts made me feel homesick: I particularly miss having someone as lovely as Gill around the place to cheer me up. It's fine when you're out filming and there are lots of distractions to keep your mind busy, but cooped up like this, you start to miss those closest to you. To make matters worse, my back is still killing me. The chiropractor paid a visit: there was a knock on the door and behind it was the biggest bloke I've ever seen, blocking out the sun as he strode in. He was built like an all-in wrestler and I was not too sure about letting him try and gently push my spine back into shape. It would be a bit like letting Giant Haystacks perform acupuncture. Anyway, I sure wasn't going to argue with him.

He unfolded his little table and popped back these little bones in the hip which he said were pressing on the sciatic nerve and causing all the pain. So it wasn't just strained muscles after all. Osteopathy's answer to Big Daddy told me that I had to keep the painful area in cold compresses and do some special exercises. I can't wait to get home and see my own physiotherapist, Don Gatherer, who has nursed me back into good condition on numerous occasions. Perhaps next time I travel I shall smuggle him around in a suitcase!

After Bone-cruncher left the room I decided that I was going to sample the delights of room service. I hadn't eaten anything for the last 24 hours except for a few grapes. My order arrived: the biggest ham sandwich I have ever seen. The baguette is well over a foot long and there is at least half a pig inside, as well as enough French fries to feed half of France. Heaven knows what the waiter thought of my room which is in an absolute mess, with clothes strewn everywhere as if the place has been ransacked by a team of lunatic burglars. I have two cases – one with my personal items and the other with gear for filming – but it is increasingly difficult to tell what belongs in what as the days go by.

What a dreadful day – without doubt the worst of the trip so far. I am cold, shivering, aching and exhausted; my back is agony; I am in a paradise I cannot enjoy; and I am worried about how things are going to pan out for the rest of the trip if we keep suffering these setbacks. And just as I was about to drift off to sleep, David Reynolds telephoned me with more bad news. The plane bringing back some of the team from another island has broken down and so we'll have to change our plans once again. Things can only get better I suppose, but at the moment it's all bloody doom and gloom.

DAY NINE

Randy the Hawaiian cowboy. Randy says he has 'the perfick' life. A more contented man I've yet to meet

THE DOCTOR WAS ABSOLUTELY RIGHT: I FEEL MUCH, MUCH BETTER. WHAT A BLOODY relief. Today we're off to see Randy the cowboy. Yes, siree, a real-life fully-fledged cowboy right here in Hawaii. And Randy is no tourist gimmick – he is as real as the horses he rides. After running cattle in Wyoming, Nevada, northern California, Arizona, Colorado – all the places where you'd expect to

The lower jaw of a wild pig

find a cowboy – Randy was approached about using his skills 3,000 miles away in the middle of the Pacific.

When we piled out of the vans somewhere high up in the hills it did not take us long to work out which one was Randy. It was as if he'd just walked straight off the set of a Western. A real Buffalo Bill, he had the chaps, the hat, the boots, the spurs and the moustache. He was a genuinely interesting character who'd been working with horses all his life; what they call a 'horse whisperer', who could tame the wildest of horses by talking to them. But he said he didn't like to be called a 'horse whisperer' and preferred to be considered simply a horse trainer.

He told us the extraordinary story of how Hawaii came to have cattle, horses and cowboys. At the beginning of the 1800s, the English sea captain George Vancouver gave the king on Big Island a gift of some cattle. Needless to say the king and the rest of the Hawaiians had never seen these strange creatures. The king was fascinated by them and ordered that they be closely guarded. Over the years the animals bred in great numbers and soon there were thousands of them running about making a nuisance of themselves. The Hawaiians were at a loss over what to do with them, when one islander said that on his travels he had seen some Mexicans riding horses and working cattle. And so it was arranged that some Mexican 'cowboys' were brought over to round up the wild animals and put them to proper use.

There's a very famous ranch here called Parker's Ranch which was established in the mid-nineteenth century and today still sprawls over a large part of the island. Randy claims that these Mexicans were the first ever cowboys and were later 'exported' to the plains on the mainland where they passed on their skills to the American settlers. Well, unlikely as it may seem that cowboys come from Hawaii, Randy sure sounded convincing enough to me …

We three in har-mon-ee, Ramsbottom, Enoch and me

Ray can't bear to look as he weighs in before boarding a light aircraft to Chuuk

Although he looked the part, Randy was no caricature of the 'hang 'em high, drink 'em dry' hard man of the Wild West. He said all that was largely a myth created and perpetuated by the Hollywood film industry. He said there has always been a much gentler side to cowboy culture which no one really knows about, and to prove it he produced a great collection of cowboy poems. 'Oh yes,' I thought, 'and now you're going to tell me that cowboys also do a bit of ballet at weekends.' But he read us one of them and I have to say I found it very moving. It was a very tender elegy about a cowboy who'd lived for his horses and loved the sound of their hooves and when he died he wanted to be buried so that they would run across his grave, and he'd be able to hear the sound of them for eternity.

Although I ceased to be surprised by anything a long time ago, one of the reasons I like America is that the culture is so vast and varied that you come across many curiosities, as well as remarkable characters like Randy the Hawaiian cowboy. It is always a thrill to have your eyes opened to something new and as we returned to our hotel in Waikiki I felt happy that Randy had reminded me that appearances can be deceptive.

THIS WAS TO BE OUR LAST NIGHT AT OUR HAWAIIAN VILLAGE HOTEL IN WAIKIKI ON the island of Oahu, before we set off early the next day for Micronesia. We had only been away for a few days but I had forgotten what a huge and extraordinary place this hotel is. Although everything your heart could possibly desire is on offer here, you certainly pay for it. One night can cost $500 – and that's just for bed and breakfast. Throw in lunch, dinner and a few drinks and you could easily run up $800 in less than 24 hours. It's scary really and you can imagine some of the high and mighty clientele they get here.

I think I preferred our stay on Big Island which was a little more unusual than Oahu. This place is not much different to Florida – just one big holiday resort. That's fine if that's all you want from your holiday but if you want something a bit different I would go for Big Island every time. I liked the variety of the landscape and weather. At sea-level you have these gorgeous, sun-kissed coasts but just a short drive up into the mountains the climate gets milder and everything gets more lush. It reminded me very much of being in the beautiful Welsh countryside with its rolling green hills and pastures, on a warm, sunny day. Then, right at the top of the mountains, there is actually snow!

Considering the island is no bigger than an English county, the diversity in ecosystems is incredible – the two sides of the island are entirely different. On one side it is like being on another planet. It is completely barren with just mile after mile of black volcanic rock and not a tree or a flower in sight. There is something awesome and eerie about the emptiness and the total absence of any form of life. The other side of the island, by contrast, is more typically Pacific and tropical with its swaying palms and exotic plants.

It's a 12-hour flight tomorrow from Honolulu to Chuuk, and this wretched trapped nerve is continuing to give me real cause for concern. I just pray that I can hold out for the rest of the trip. Tomorrow will be a crucial day: if my back gets any worse then the whole project will be in jeopardy, but if I can make it through such a long flight then I will be confident of lasting the whole trip. Fingers crossed.

25c
BY ROYAL LETTERS PATENT

PART TWO – MICRONESIA

DAY TEN

TODAY WE LEAVE HAWAII AND HEAD THOUSANDS OF MILES ACROSS THE VAST PACIFIC to the tiny island of Chuuk in Micronesia. Chuuk (called Truk until recently) is best known as the place where the United States exacted a terrible revenge on the Japanese for the assault on Pearl Harbor. The massive Japanese Combined Fleet, as well as hundreds of aeroplanes and tens of thousands of troops, were based in Chuuk's 38-mile long natural lagoon. It was known as the 'Gibraltar of the Pacific' because of its strategic military importance in the area. From there the Japanese were able to control much of South-east Asia, Indonesia and the South Pacific. In 1944, in one of the heaviest bombardments in the history of aerial warfare, American bombers pounded their targets for 36 hours, sinking dozens of ships and seriously undermining Japan's military capacity in the Pacific.

Today, the wrecks of the Japanese fleet litter the floor of the lagoon and create one of the most awesome diving sites in the world. I have heard so much about Chuuk from other divers down the years and it has always been one of my dreams to go there. Now, thanks to this programme, I have got the chance and my only worry is that my expectations are so high that I may be disappointed.

Hawaii has been a fabulous experience but we have been here for nearly 10 days and we are all feeling excited about the prospect of going to somewhere genuinely remote. For all its natural beauty and various charms, there is no hiding the fact that Hawaii is very touristy. We have been living fairly luxuriously here but our researcher Judy has warned us that Chuuk will be pretty spartan, even a little rough, by comparison.

As we headed out to Honolulu airport, we drove past desolate expanses of volcanic rock. These great sheets of undulating cooled lava have been decorated by 'natural' graffiti artists who have spelt their names with white pebbles taken from the beach.

After a now familiar breakfast of scrambled eggs, sausages, hash browns, orange juice and cappuccino at Stingrays burger bar in the airport, we clamber aboard our plane for the next stage on our epic journey. We will be travelling through the international date line, which means losing a day from our lives. I can't quite understand how this works, but if I can get my head round it by the end of the flight I'll let you know. What I do know is that if we were travelling the other way then we would take off today and arrive yesterday! Work that one out.

From the air the Hawaiian islands look like a string of sparkling pearls embedded in turquoise glass. I never tire of the thrill of looking out of an aeroplane window and marvelling at the natural beauty of the planet. As I mentioned earlier, I always wanted to be a spaceman and I suppose this is about as close as I am ever going to get. After a short while all I could see was

The Blue Lagoon at Chuuk

A desert island in Chuuk Lagoon

hundreds of miles of blue, blue ocean and blue, blue skies with a scattering of tiny little clouds shining radiantly in the sun. It looks absolutely stunning.

Our imaginations are incapable of picturing the sheer size of the world's oceans, but flying for hours and hours over the Pacific in daylight filled me with a sense of wonder. And as we sped over it at about 500 m.p.h., I thought how impregnably vast these seas must have seemed to the first explorers from Europe. It would often be several months before the likes of Cook and his crew saw land as they sailed slowly through endless ocean.

After we've been in the air for about an hour, we are served breakfast, and guess what it is? Scrambled eggs, sausages, hash browns, orange juice and coffee. 'Quelle surprise!' as they say in Paris. I decided to save myself for lunch. I use the term 'lunch' in the loosest possible sense as it turned out to be a dead sandwich – two bits of bread with a filling of indeterminate origin.

After five hours we touched down on a tiny pinprick of land called Jensen Island, a solitary outcrop of rock, which seems to sport nothing much more than a runway and a couple of out-buildings. Once again, my back had locked and it took me about five minutes to stand up – so much for the physiotherapy skills of the sumo wrestler. I wanted to go outside and exercise my stupid back, so I was relieved when the door opened and a beautiful blast of hot air rushed in. But it turned out that we were not allowed to leave the plane as Jensen is a military base used by the US air force and security is strict. I suppose we could have put our hands on our hips and said, 'Do you have any idea of how far we have come ...?', but I guess they would have had a pretty good idea. So I grabbed my exercise by walking up and down the aisle of the plane, looking like an older, more tanned version of the Hunchback of Notre-Dame.

Some closely cropped soldiers got off the plane and were replaced by some others, all sporting the same bullet-head hairdos (they tell me it's very trendy at the moment). Take-off was clearly going to need all the pilot's skill and all the plane's power. We taxied as far as we possibly could to one end of the strip. Under the starboard wing (that's the right one for you ground lubbers) I could see the ocean just a few feet away. I had noticed when we were doing our crosswind leg to prepare for a landing, just how short the runway really was. If it was 50 metres or so shorter you probably would not be able to generate enough speed to lift off. The pilot wound up the throttle so that the engines were shrieking and I have to confess to feeling a little nervous when he finally released the brakes, the seat punched me in the back and we began to hurtle down the runway. But just when I began to think that we must be only seconds away from careering into the sea I got that strange feeling in my stomach – like you get going over a humped-back bridge at speed – and I knew we were airborne.

We stopped off at other islands along the way, dropping off some deliveries and picking up others – it must be the longest postal round in the world. As we get closer to Micronesia the islands become more tropically verdant and look beautiful from the air. One island we passed was very mountainous and as I looked out of the aircraft I saw rain lashing down on one side while the other was basking in glorious sunshine. If the rain in Spain stays mainly in the plain, then in the Pacific it is specific, which is terrific, but in Chuuk it's enough to make you ... on second thoughts, I don't think I'll pursue that one.

K INTERNATIONAL AIRPORT.

These weren't quite the famous wrecks we had been expecting to find on Chuck

MICRONESIA IS A GROUP OF ABOUT 2,000 ISLANDS JUST NORTH OF THE EQUATOR AND all but about 120 of them are inhabited. The islands themselves are all small – none of them much bigger than the Isle of Wight – but they are spread over 1,800 miles running east to west and 600 miles north to south. According to Judy, our encyclopaedic researcher, the total area covered by Micronesia is about 4.5 million square miles, which is roughly the size of the United States. If the area was superimposed on Europe and Asia it would stretch from the British Isles to Iran. But of that, only about 1,200 square miles is made up of land – an area not much bigger than Luxembourg. The rest is just ocean. As Michael Caine once said: 'Not a lot of people know that!'

Apparently, in the 1520s the great Portuguese explorer Ferdinand Magellan was the first European to reach the islands, during his incredible circumnavigation of the world. Hearing about the details of that voyage made me realize how luxurious and convenient modern travel is by comparison. By the time his ships had crossed the Atlantic and rounded Cape Horn into the Pacific the crew was living in the most appalling conditions. Much of their food had been devoured by worms and other insects, and the water smelt so bad that the sailors held their noses as they drank it. Rats and even leather became a delicacy. (But would they have dared eat our dubious looking in-flight sandwich? I suspect that they were not that desperate.) Magellan originally named the islands 'Los Ladrones', meaning 'The Isles of Thieves', after some of the islanders stole a skiff belonging to one of his six ships.

After crossing the international date line and losing a day of our lives we began to descend through the mist and rain-clouds to touch down at Chuuk airport on the main island of Weno. When I say 'airport' I am perhaps being misleading – Heathrow it is not. It is a strip of concrete and a shed with about

Waiting at Chuuk airport for our luggage – which is 5,000 miles away in Hawaii

Meeting the locals at the fish market

two official-looking officials. Bad news greets us in the shed when we are told by the Two Ronnies that most of our luggage failed to join us on the flight, which means no cameras, no equipment, no change of clothes. My possessions consist of the trousers I am standing up in, or more accurately, standing inside of.

When we enquired why we were here and our baggage was sitting on the other side of the world, we were told that it was too heavy and would arrive on another flight at some unspecified point in the future. I am sure I saw an evil smile appear on the faces of the Two Ronnies as they expressed their hopes that our baggage would make the trip. I don't know whether you have ever travelled a quarter of the way around the planet in a cramped, uncomfortable plane with terrible food and a blocked toilet, only to be told by a grinning gauleiter that your bags are lost … Well, let me just say that little Ronnie came as close as anyone I've met in recent years to 'swallowing his teeth'.

Travelling from the airport to our hotel was a real eye-opener. The inhabitants may be living on a beautiful tropical island, but this sure isn't paradise. Many of the locals live like animals and it was dreadful to see. We saw dozens of squalid little huts made from assorted bits of timber and metal, all of them surrounded by piles of rubbish. We saw little kids playing barefoot in burnt-out cars. There are more vehicle wrecks strewn along the roadside than there are cars driving on the road. We were all quite shocked by what we saw, except for Judy who had visited the islands a few months earlier on her research trip and knew what to expect. When we were told we were coming to see the famous wrecks of Chuuk, this wasn't quite what I had had in mind. Despite all the garbage on the ground, Chuuk enjoys some of the cleanest air on earth as there are no industrialized, heavily polluted areas within thousands of miles of the islands.

Henry, our driver, who has lived on the islands all his life, explained to us why there was so much poverty. The average annual wage of the Chuukese is about $2,000 (about £1,300) and for many years the islands' biggest source of revenue has been grants from the US government. There is barely an economy to speak of and about two thirds of the Chuukese population are employed by the government. What real economy there is is based on subsistence fishing and farming. Coconut is the main cash crop, but breadfruit, yams, bananas and sweet potatoes are also produced – mainly just for local consumption. Tourism also brings in some money, but the remoteness of the islands and the lack of facilities and comfort mean that almost all the visitors are diving enthusiasts.

A local making leis from aromatic petals and leaves

Ironically, Chuuk was once thought to be something of a potential goldmine. When Germany bought the islands from Spain for a few million pesetas at the end of the last century, they thought they had just pulled off a very astute deal. The Germans were interested in copra – the dried flesh of the coconut – which could be refined into a much sought-after oil. It was considered so precious that it was known as 'Micronesian gold', but a sequence of devastating typhoons and mysterious diseases in the trees meant that the Germans barely saw any return on their investment before Japan seized the islands about 20 years later.

We all felt pretty low as we headed to our hotel. We were tired, our luggage and equipment were still in Hawaii, and we felt depressed by the sight of so much terrible poverty. We were told that there are only about 200 hotel rooms in the whole of Chuuk and that we should not expect too much. My only hope was that there would be air-conditioning as the heat and the humidity there is almost overwhelming. And so there was: a fan over my bed that did about two revolutions an hour. I lay on my bed and opened up my guide-book on Micronesia. The first sentence I read tells me that there are 7,000 different varieties of insects in Micronesia. By the sound of buzzing around me it seems I am going to be spending the night with about half of them. Marvellous.

DAY ELEVEN

Ready, Steady, Chuuk! Alanasia Aliwis lays out the ingredients for her magic love potion

BUT IS IT DAY 11? IS IT NOT 12 AS WE MISSED A WHOLE DAY IN THE BLINK OF AN EYE? Maybe it's day 10 all over again? I am confused. Either way, we've been here about 36 hours and our clothes and most of our equipment are still nowhere to be seen. We are starting to smell, especially Ray. The airline has given us a voucher for some clothes, but needless to say Chuuk High Street is not exactly brimming with international fashion houses. Judy searched high and low before coming back with some really naff shorts and shirts. We're going to look like a poor imitation of the Beach Boys.

I've started to take painkillers for the ache in my leg, which seems to have been caused by the problem in my back. I don't normally like taking pills, but the pain has become really quite bad since we arrived. When we get to Guam, I will go and see a specialist and hope that he has a little more success than Giant Haystacks. I hope I haven't done any permanent damage, but I suppose you always fear the worst when you are away from home.

Despite the fact that most of our kit was probably going round and round the baggage carousel in Oslo or Mexico City, we still managed to do some filming with the one camera and the bit of sound equipment that somehow made it on to the plane with the people it belonged to. (Like a good boy scout, Corky is always well prepared.) We did a scene with this extraordinary local lady called Alanasia Aliwis, who was a witch and proud of it. When she wasn't selling fruit from her market stall, she was busy concocting her secret love

Henry explains the wonders of the love stick

Testing the power of my love stick on a local woman

potion which was made up of all sorts of weird ingredients. Her brew was supposed to have special magical powers.

A person was meant to spit or sprinkle the potion on the object of their devotion and, hey presto!, the person fell completely in love with them. Mind you, I'm not too sure how I would feel if a woman walked up and spat some evil-smelling gook all over me. I have to confess that my first reaction would not be to jump into her arms and swear undying love. Swear, yes . . . Still, perhaps that's where the magic comes in. Mind you, if it was Nicole Kidman . . .

We were also shown an item of local handicraft known as 'the Chuuk love-stick'. Although nowadays they are little more than an amusing curiosity for tourists, it was not long ago that every man in Chuuk possessed one of these extraordinary objects. They are about six feet long and were used by the man to test whether a girl wanted to make love to him. He would push the stick through the grass wall of the hut of the girl he desired and he would then entangle her hair with it. If the girl pulled it, then that meant he could come in; if she shook it, then it meant that she was coming out; but if she pushed it away, then she was rejecting him. Apparently the girl could tell who the stick belonged to by feeling the amount of ribs and notches on it. As you can imagine, there were one or two 'industrial' jokes cracked amongst the crew as we inspected these local artefacts. The highly witty repartee went something like this:

'I bet if Ray pushed it through the hut he'd get her mother.'

'More like her brother.'

'I think he'd get the father – Ray likes an older man.'

'Ray would be happy enough with the stick …'

Etc, etc … Poor old Ray.

There was another highly amusing moment that day, provided by who else but … Ray. When we popped over to one of the neighbouring islands our dive guru stepped off the boat clutching his two-way radio. Unfortunately, Ray stepped not on to the land side like the rest of us but straight into the 'sea side'. As he disappeared under water he managed to keep his precious radio above his head as if he was starring in a scene from *Excalibur*. It was some time before our dive guru dried out and even longer before the final laughter amongst the crew died away. It's frightening to think that this man was a highly respected soldier in some of Britain's crack regiments. Ah, maybe it was cracked regiments …

Discovering the truth about my designer label

WITH THE LOST LUGGAGE SAGA showing no sign of being resolved Mike Treen, the producer, got in on the shopping act, clearly unhappy about tramping around looking like a Beach Boy. He went into a local village and returned with an equally garish set of clothes – and some Y-fronts for the whole crew! Mindful of my mother's wise words about not wanting to be embarrassed if I was knocked down by a bus, I did actually change into a fresh pair of underwear. I also put on a beige T-shirt with SDA emblazoned on the pocket. I imagined that SDA was the logo of some trendy American Pacific designer label. Anton was wearing exactly the same shirt and shorts, and as we toddled off together, looking like Tweedledum and Tweedledee, we soon discovered that we had become the object of widespread hilarity among the local population. When a local woman and her young daughter collapsed into fits of laughter at the sight of us, we asked them what was so funny. The little girl, trying to conceal her

Native dancers at Blue Lagoon

Stop! Only men in grass skirts allowed in here

giggles, informed us that we were wearing the local school uniform, a place run by the Seventh Day Adventists. The comedy fashion show continues.

For our evening meal, we decided to order crab. When you are on a small island in the middle of nowhere surrounded by an ocean the size of the United States, it is a fairly safe bet that the seafood is going to be the safest choice on the menu. The waters around here are teeming with sea bass, tuna, mullet, lobsters, shrimps, clams and oysters. But we decide to go for crab because we had seen a Japanese couple being served one last night and it was massive and looked absolutely delicious. Its legs hung so far over the side of the plate it looked as if it had walked to the table.

Our order was taken by a very nice Chuukese girl who spoke quite good English, even though her cockney rhyming slang was a little rusty. In my loudest voice – it's funny how we think that the louder we talk to foreigners the better they will understand – I said I wanted the same as the Japanese couple last night. Mr Reynolds then butted in to point out that I couldn't have the *same* as the Japanese couple as they had already eaten it and that what I really wanted was something similar. I don't know what the Chuukese for 'smart alec' is but the poor girl finally got there in the end. But when our 'giant' crab arrived it turned out to be about the size of a 10p piece and it had only got one claw. I imagined saying to the waitress, 'Excuse me, why has this crab only got one claw?', to which she would of course reply, 'I'm sorry sir, but he's been in a fight', leaving me open for the stunningly original comic riposte: 'Well, why don't you bring me the winner?' Exit stage left to tumultuous applause.

DAY TWELVE

I'D BEEN IN THE VERY DEEPEST OF SLEEPS BEFORE I SAT BOLT UPRIGHT IN BED, having been woken up by the most almighty clanging and banging. I looked at my watch: six o'clock. It was time for breakfast (and to think I had only just got over the trauma of my last brush with Chuukese cuisine). The alarm call here does not take the form of a light rapping of the knuckles on sir's door nor a cheery phone call from reception. The noise reminds me of those old Western movies where they have a big triangle outside the eating house and the cook comes out in a funny hat and apron and bangs it with a big iron bar. There is also a good incentive to get there by 6.30 – the tapioca and omelette will be cold and solid. Not the brightest way to start the day. Hot or cold, however, the tapioca and omelette will taste of one thing: paraffin, the fuel used in the stoves. Yum, my favourite.

I felt a little tense as I ate breakfast, contemplating my first deep dive in three or four years. But I also felt a great sense of excitement about the prospect of doing one of the world's truly great dives. The wrecks, about 60 of them as well as a number of aircraft, are spread all over the lagoon, so we will be making several dives. The main dive is planned for the freighter the *San Francisco Maru* at about 170 feet.

Denis searches for some blue sky, watched by Anton and David Reynolds

I should explain why these deep dives can be a little nerve-racking. As you descend you enter what is known as 'blue water' at about 60 to 70 feet down, where the light is the same above as it is below and to the sides so you don't know which way is up or down. This can be a very disturbing experience and it has been known to cause some divers to panic. Light in water undergoes a strange transformation. Colours are slowly filtered out as you descend until there is nothing but blackness. Even in clear waters reds, for example, turn to greens at about five metres (a couple of years ago I cut myself on a broken bottle during a deep dive and although the wound was not too bad it was a little alarming to look at your blood and discover that it is green!)

Diving among the wrecks of the Japanese fleet in Chuuk Lagoon

Most objects lose their natural colour. Artificial light, therefore, is needed to bring out the colours as well as to guide you through the pitch darkness deeper down.

Water also does strange things to sound. Sound is transmitted much quicker under water than on land, with the difference that you cannot tell what direction it is coming from. But far from being a silent world as you might think, it can be pretty noisy under water. I have heard sea creatures crunching on coral. It sounds like a family eating cornflakes without milk.

Moreover, I was thinking about the history of the place and anticipating what we were going to find down there. The attack on Chuuk Lagoon was one of the key episodes of the struggle in the Pacific during World War Two. The islands had been occupied by Japan since 1914, but after the Chuuk raid, known as Operation Hailstone, the Allies gradually took control of them, amid some of the fiercest fighting of the whole war. The Japanese had won few friends during the hostilities in these islands. Rape and mass murder of locals were common and at the war crimes trials at the end of the conflict the Japanese were accused of practising cannibalism on American and Australian soldiers.

When the Japanese were preparing for the war they secretly moved 40,000 troops into this remote lagoon, building airfields and submarine pens as part of a giant military base. The passes into the lagoon were mined and defended by big artillery guns making it almost completely safe from sea attack. The only possible threat was from the air, and that's where the Americans came from on the morning of 17 February 1944 as they darkened the skies with wave upon wave of aircraft. Operation Hailstone went on for 36 hours and over 60 vessels were sunk – some of them by submarines at the mouth of the harbour as they tried to escape. Never before or since have so many ships been sunk in a single action. The damage would have been even greater if the Japanese had not spotted a US reconnaissance flight 10 days earlier which gave the admirals time to move some of the fleet beyond the probable reach of the bombers.

Today, the lagoon is a giant open war museum and I am not exaggerating when I say that diving in it was one of the greatest experiences of my life.

OUR FIRST DIVE WAS TO BE TO THE *SAN FRANCISCO MARU*. SHORTLY AFTER OUR BOAT arrived at the point directly above it, myself, Gradvin, the local dive-master, and Ray, who was to operate the camera, silently slid into the water. We were all feeling a bit nervous and we knew we had to have our wits about us going to such depths. Wrecks can be dangerous if you get stuck or lost in one of the many dark corners or corridors of their giant structures. Yesterday we were told about an American film crew who visited Chuuk a few years ago and who never returned to the surface after they got lost inside one of the ships and ran out of air.

We slowly went down the anchor-line and through the 'blue water' to about 60 feet, where we checked on each other to see that we were all okay. When diving, it is not just returning to the surface too quickly that you have to avoid. Descending can also be dangerous as you can burst an eardrum if you go too fast and fail to 'equalize', as it is known, with the surrounding water pressure. This happens when divers get overexcited about the sight of a beautiful coral reef or a fascinating wreck. It is true to say that the biggest danger under water is not sharks but pressure. For those not familiar with its dangers, here is a brief explanation.

The deeper under water you go, the greater is the pressure exerted on your body from all sides. As the human body is 70 per cent water, this pressure does not have too drastic an effect on the body itself, but it does on the air that goes down with the diver and is passed into the lungs. Why, you may ask, is this dangerous? The danger can be demonstrated by taking an inflated balloon below water: the air inside will become compressed and as you descend, the balloon will become smaller and shrink altogether as the pressure increases. As you return to the surface the balloon returns to its original size as it re-inflates. This, therefore, is what happens to your lungs. So, in order for your lungs to operate normally they must be supplied with air at the same pressure as the surrounding water, i.e., compressed air. The regulator on the aqua-lung ensures the pressure is right. The deeper you go, the denser and more compressed the air you breathe, and therefore you get through your supply much quicker when diving deep. At 20 metres, for example, you breathe three times more air than at the surface. Right, that's the science lesson over. Did you get all that at the back?

After our slow descent we left the safety of the anchor-line, following

Gradvin as we gradually headed into the gloom. Slowly a very, very eerie shape came into focus. It was the *San Francisco*, in all its ghostly wonder, lying upright with her keel on the floor of the lagoon and her deck completely level as if she was sitting on a very calm sea. The gloomy visibility made it doubly eerie but if she had been on her side or tilted at angle I don't think the sight would have been nearly so arresting. She looked strangely untroubled. As we moved along her massive deck, which is now largely covered in coral, we looked to the starboard side and saw two tanks in near-pristine condition leaning precariously over the edge. On top of one of the tanks was a Buddha which had been placed there by the Japanese in 1988 in honour of their dead.

We were now about 170 feet under water and we had a quick get-together to monitor our situation as any oversights on our part or equipment malfunctions could be fatal. One cock-up at this depth and it's the long goodnight. Everything was in order so we pressed on. Next we came across the forward hold and when we entered it my heart leapt as I saw dozens and dozens of sea mines. They are huge great metal balls with spikes all around just like the ones you see in the old war films. Next to them were boxes of ammunition, hand-grenades and shells; every conceivable weapon that you could imagine, just lying there a few feet away from us, full, presumably, of tons of explosives. I felt a distinct sense of relief when we moved on.

We went past the deck and the rigging into a second massive hold where we were met by an even more extraordinary sight. There were huge lorries and

what looked like petrol tankers, as well as motorcycles and other bits of machinery that we couldn't make out in the gloom. This was incredible. Unlike most wrecks, the *San Francisco* is fully intact and its cargo is loaded just as it would have been on the day it was holed by the American torpedo-bombers.

I felt very emotional as I tried to imagine those terrifying final few minutes of life experienced by those on board. I imagined the sailors on deck, going about their daily routine in glorious sunshine and then bang: an almighty explosion, the deck rocks, alarms sound, gunfire all around, fires break loose, the ocean begins to pour in and there is pandemonium as the crew run this way and that. The ship then begins to list and slides beneath the water as the screams of the men trapped below slowly die out.

We have been down just 12 minutes when our computer tells us it's time to return to the surface. We have been so deep that we've raced through our air supply in next to no time. This is deeply frustrating. I would love to explore this giant war museum-cum-graveyard for much, much longer, but we must now decompress on the way up – a process that takes longer than our actual dive.

We stop at 60 feet, 30 feet and 20 feet for five-minute decompression stops. I check my air at 20 feet and notice it's getting quite low, but there is just enough to allow another stop at 15 feet for three minutes, which I must complete otherwise there is a danger of getting 'the bends'.

The bends is another major hazard facing the diver. For those not familiar

Myself and Gradvin inspect the plaque laid by the Japanese on the deck of the Fujikawa Maru, *while Jim films us*

An old shell on a coral-encrusted deck

Getting into the cockpit of the Betty Bomber

A guru through the looking glass. Ray about to enter the bomber through a gun port

with diving, when a diver goes deep, a large amount of nitrogen builds up in the blood in liquid form. If you surface too rapidly, the sudden reduction in pressure means that the excess nitrogen will not have time to be absorbed slowly into the body. This causes bubbles to form as the nitrogen returns to gas and they become trapped in your blood stream and body tissues. The bubbles expand as you surface and block blood circulation and damage your nervous system. This is called decompression sickness, or 'the bends', and if the flow of blood to the head or heart is blocked then the result will be death or paralysis. Thankfully, we have done our sums right and we reach the surface with enough air left to allow for any unforeseen setbacks in our ascent.

After more than the recommended surface interval we made a shallow dive to see the wrecked ship, the *Fujikawa Maru*. It was a strange feeling to move through the galley and see cups and saucers still waiting to be used, and bottles of beer and saki still unopened. We also saw the Betty Bomber, its pilot seat intact and many of the controls in place. Being made of aluminium, even fifty years in the sea has not caused it to rust.

By now we were running late and there was not time to visit one of the most famous wrecks in Chuuk Lagoon.

The I-169 was the pride of the Japanese fleet and was sunk six weeks after the main American raids. During another air attack, the sub began to crash-dive but one of her crew had forgotten to close one of the valves and the control-room became flooded. As the vessel, with its entire crew trapped inside, was unable to surface, a diver was sent down and reported that he heard responses to his hammer signal. After a number of abortive attempts to lift her, it was decided that there was nothing that could be done and so the vessel was abandoned and those inside left to die a slow death. Some of the bodies were later recovered before the sub was quickly depth-charged to ensure that the approaching American forces would have no benefit from it. Twenty years later, an American diver called Al Giddings made Chuuk Lagoon famous when he managed to enter the sub and film Japanese skeletons in uniform floating around in the water.

I dearly wanted to see the sub myself but instead we had to head back to shore. As we took off our equipment, the three of us said very little. We were all in little worlds of our own as we tried to digest the amazing images we had just seen. All those people who had assured me down the years that Chuuk Lagoon is a truly unforgettable dive were not exaggerating. Even as I write this later in the evening, when the adrenaline has had plenty of time to subside, I can honestly say that today's dive is probably one of the most emotional and rewarding I have ever made. It was awe-inspiring in the truest sense and I would be extremely surprised if I ever make another dive like it.

DAY THIRTEEN

I SPENT MOST OF THE NIGHT WRITHING AROUND WITH THE MOST HORRENDOUS indigestion or food poisoning, or both. I suppose some problem of this sort is only to be expected when in exotic locations. As I lay there groaning and wrestling with my sheet I tried to work out what might have caused it, as I had gone to bed in the best of spirits. I had sat out on the balcony admiring the incredible night skies you get in this part of the world. The air here is so clean that there is nothing in the atmosphere fuzzing up your view of the stars. It's as if a giant window framing the heavens has been given a once-over with a bit of spit and polish.

About an hour later I began to feel as if my stomach had been filled with sulphuric acid. To be honest, the food here in Chuuk is not great, but that is not altogether surprising somewhere as remote as this. Chefs (if they exist at

DIVE
TRUK LAGOON
SPAM
SPAM
Hormel

all) can hardly just nip out the back door to Harrods food hall. The natural produce is limited to fresh fish and a few fruits – and besides, trying to eke out a living is hard enough for the locals. Understandably, *haute cuisine* is not top of the list of priorities when you are taking home about $40 a week, if you're lucky.

My tin of Spam – a purchase I was later to regret

As I lay there with these terrible cramps, it dawned on me that the cause might have nothing to do with the local cuisine and everything to do with an early evening snack I had taken with David Reynolds. He had come over to my room clutching a half-bottle of champagne the management had given him. I remembered that we had bought a tin of Spam earlier in the day as part of a gag for the filming and so we sat there admiring the glorious sunset over the lagoon, quaffing champagne and munching on Spam with a bit of tomato sauce, which I'd smuggled out of the aircraft. It tasted delicious at the time, but a few hours later it occurred to me that perhaps champagne and Spam weren't quite designed to complement each other! However, I was soon to learn that the saga of my stomach was not the only excitement of the night.

Far from it. Denis, the cameraman, had a far more unappetizing story to tell. In the middle of the night he was woken up by an intruder who had climbed on to his balcony on the ground floor and through an open window into his room. (It is so hot here and the medieval cooling systems are of so little help that you have to keep the windows open to avoid being microwaved in your sleep.) Being the good, phlegmatic Brit that he is, Denis stood his ground and demanded to know what on earth his unwanted visitor was doing in his room. The Chuukese robber said that he wanted five dollars. Denis, standing there wearing nothing more than the outfit God had given him at birth, told the robber to get on his way – though perhaps not quite so politely.

Alarmed by Denis's tough bargaining position – or more likely the sight of him in the buff – our frustrated robber reduced his demands to three dollars. But still Denis refused to budge from his position of zero tolerance. (We are not talking a lot of money here, but principles are principles.) 'Okay, make it one dollar,' came the final plea. Denis was not open to persuasion and so the robber, looking a little put out by his spectacular failure to extract even a dime from his victim, left the way he came. Unfortunately for our intrepid local hero he fell over the balcony in the manner of Inspector Clouseau and straight into the arms of a pair of security guards who just happened to be coming round the corner for a quiet smoke. He was handcuffed and led away. If it was to the local jail then the young man can take with him my most sincere commiserations. The hotels are bad enough.

That morning, news of another unpleasant confrontation with the local population came to light. Yesterday, Mike Treen, our producer, took some of the crew off to try and film a scene with some locals performing a ritual battle dance. Mike had negotiated a price with the chief man of the outfit and then filmed the sequence.

When it was over, the chief suddenly and aggressively announced that he wanted an improved appearance fee, far in excess of the one originally agreed. And that was not all: the burly bigwig also wanted royalties when the programme was shown back in the UK! Mike's negotiating position was easy to understand – he had just two words to pass on to the man and they were not, suffice it to say, 'Merry' and 'Christmas'. But the chief is not for backing down.

Mike Treen waiting to be posted home at Chuuk Airport before the flight to Australia

He's been to Europe, he knows the world of showbiz, he tells Mike, growing more and more aggressive as 'the contract talks' continue. Finally, our normally patient and reasonable producer stomps across to the camera, rips it open, takes the tape out of the cassette, throws it on the floor, treads on it and says, 'There you are, you can take your bloody dancers and stuff them in a place where the sun don't shine.' I wasn't there unfortunately. It would have been worth a good deal of my fee to see mild-mannered Mike jump up and down on a film cassette.

The locals by and large had been a pretty friendly crew. We had been told before arriving that other Micronesians think the Chuukese are often aggressive and rude, but that was not our experience. Henry, our driver, told us that the only time we should be on our guard was on Friday and Saturday nights when Chuuk men like to go out and drink heavily. The worst nights apparently are on government pay-days, the second and fourth Fridays in the month, when everyone rushes out to spend their hard-earned. He said the violence can be quite frightening at times as Chuukese men – most of whom seem pretty powerfully built – will often batter each other to the bitter end. Sounds a bit like any high street in Britain on a Friday night, if you ask me.

WE ARE LEAVING FOR GUAM IN A COUPLE OF HOURS AND FIRST I MUST DEVOTE MYSELF to my favourite pastime – packing. Our much travelled kit had finally made it to Chuuk – God only knows where it had been – and it was here just long enough for the entire contents of both my cases to be strewn across my hotel room as if a typhoon had passed through.

The little airport on Weno has got nothing in it except a tiny bar run by a tiny woman who stands there with her eyeballs peering over the counter like Mr Chad or Kilroy. It is more of a potting shed than an airport, but airports being airports we still had to book in two hours prior to our flight and then, of course, there is my second favourite travel pastime – processing! It seemed especially ridiculous when we were the only people in the airport apart from the miniature barmaid.

A beady-eyed official, dressed up like a traffic warden, looked us up and down and stared meaningfully at our documents. I am sure it is all just an act. Your passport could carry a picture of Basil Brush and these officials would stare at it, then at you, then back at the photo and then hand it back with that special tough guy's nod of the head that only airport personnel can do. Our battle with bureaucracy over, we spend the next hour and a half just wandering about in the sweltering heat. I was dripping in sweat and rarely have I been so desperate to get on an aeroplane.

Although I can say with complete confidence that I will miss neither our hotel nor the airport, I was sad to leave Chuuk itself. The French have a saying that in every goodbye there is a mild sense of death, a vague feeling of loss. As our plane climbed steeply into the brilliant blue sky I looked back on that strange, wild, beautiful place and realized that I would probably never return. There are other destinations and other challenges and not enough time for them all. When I get back to England, the dreadful food and shoddy hotel will have passed from my memory but I will never forget my dive in Chuuk – even if I live a thousand years.

TELEVISION

White

PART THREE – AUSTRALIA

DAY FOURTEEN

Rodney Fox shows me the jawbone of a great white shark – the beast that almost killed him

ONCE AGAIN ON THIS TRIP WE FOUND OURSELVES VEERING FROM ONE EXTREME TO another. When we arrived in Guam at about seven in the evening, we were picked up by mini-buses and whisked off to the luxurious Hilton Hotel where the contrast with our basic accommodation in Chuuk could not be starker. It feels as if we are back in Hawaii. I've got a television that would not look out of place in some cinemas. I could fit two football pitches in my bedroom and still have space for the fans. The air-conditioning is so effective you need a woolly jumper to walk around in. From my balcony I've got a stunning view of the sea and I can see huge curling waves crashing in on the shore.

We are not here in Guam long enough to explore it properly (only 24 hours before we move on to Cairns and one of the wonders of the natural world – the Great Barrier Reef), but I was immediately struck by how westernized it felt compared to Chuuk. The buildings are modern, the wide urban streets are busy with people and cars, the water is drinkable and there are thousands of 'western' faces around. Most of them are servicemen, based at the massive US naval base, who seem to have transported American culture, wholesale, to the island.

Before dinner we got chatting to a couple of off-duty naval officers in the bar who told us some fascinating stories about the US territory. Although it is only a small island, 50 miles long and 5 to 10 miles wide, Guam is crucial to America's military strategy in the Far East. It was the scene of some of the most ferocious fighting in World War Two as well as some acts of the greatest bravery and heroism. After American marines stormed the beaches here in 1944, the Japanese launched wave after wave of suicidal counterattacks. Both sides lost over 60 per cent of their troops in the engagements, which often came down to hand-to-hand fighting. The Americans held their ground but several pockets of Japanese troops broke through to the back of the US line where they were resisted by a motley assortment of cooks, clerks and even patients. We were also told that it was here in Guam that a Japanese corporal emerged from the jungle and surrendered to the Americans – in 1972!

Later that evening we met a group of American conservationists who were on a fact-finding mission. The facts they were finding seemed pretty alarming. They told us that Guam was in danger of becoming the first significant land mass on earth to lose all its indigenous bird-life. The cause, for once, is not man's hunting or pollution, but a six-foot-long tree-climbing snake which was accidentally introduced to the islands when one or two of them hitched a ride on a US plane or ship during the war. Now there are hundreds of thousands of them living on the island and feasting themselves on their favourite delicacies – birds' eggs and chicks. The guy told us that if all the birds were wiped out, it would have a devastating impact on the island's entire ecological structure, affecting the insect population and thus the pollination of the island's plants.

DAY FIFTEEN

TODAY HAS BEEN SOMETHING OF A NON-EVENT, ONE OF THOSE 'FILLER' DAYS NECESSARY on a long trip. I won't bore you with the details: I had a shave and a shower, took breakfast, packed my wash-bag, drank a Coke, stared at the wall, mooched around the hotel and set off to the airport from where we flew to Cairns in north-eastern Australia. But here's an interesting fact for you. There are 10 of us on the trip carrying 64 items of luggage. I know this little statistic very well by now because every time we go to an airport (I can barely bring myself to utter the dreaded 'A' word) we count them out at one end and count them back in at the other – just like the reporter in the Falklands War with the RAF Harriers, though not quite so exciting or heroic.

It was the same again at Cairns airport where we counted in the 52 boxes of film kit and our 12 items of personal luggage. The process felt particularly laborious on this occasion as it was shortly after midnight that our flight arrived. I hope to be able to bring you more enlightening and entertaining news tomorrow. 'G'night possums', as they say in these parts.

Over the trip I became very familiar with our 64 items of luggage

DAY SIXTEEN

I open my curtains and lay eyes on Cairns for the first time in daylight. On first impressions it looks like a seaside resort. There are several yachts bobbing around in the harbour and people bustling around on the quayside as they prepare to head off to the Great Barrier Reef for diving and snorkelling. I have a wonderful view of the mountains across the bay, which are draped in great woolly clouds and thick with rainforest on the higher reaches. The weather seems to be very mild here and nothing like as hot and humid as Guam or Chuuk. Apparently it's been bucketing down for the last week or so but it doesn't look too disastrous to me. I wish I could say the same about my suitcase.

It would not be possible to arrange a greater mess if I took a whole day off to do it. There are dirty clothes, clean clothes, pills, more pills, bits of paper, fugitive items from my wash-bag, books, odd shoes, a kitchen sink, an armchair ... It appears to have developed an ecosystem all of its own. Rogue socks are developing signs of life. By the time we get back to Heathrow I will probably be able to plant small seeds and saplings in there. When I get home, rather than try and unpack it I will just dump it on the lawn and watch it turn into a garden feature.

We've only got a couple of hours off before we fly on again to Lizard Island, where we stay for a few days before returning to this hotel here in Cairns. To book into a hotel and then move straight out may not sound like the most logical course of action, but believe me it makes perfect logistical sense. Well, according to Judy and Mike's masterplan it does.

I decided to ignore my suitcases (attention-seekers that they are) and went for breakfast. Afterwards I strolled around the corner to the post office and changed my US dollars into Australian ones before taking a brief diversion to explore the town. The swaying palms and lush vegetation give Cairns a very tropical feel, but it definitely has a character and charm all of its own. I don't know why but I was expecting it be more American in style. Maybe that's because everywhere we have been so far has been either a part of the States or a dependent territory.

American culture is fairly uniform: everyone seems to wear baseball caps, shorts and trainers while burgers, pizzas and cold beers or Cokes fill most restaurant menus. But here everything seems a bit more low-key and less garish. There's a lot of nice-looking family-run restaurants and snack bars and not too many Wendy burger joints or flashing neon signs. Still, I've yet to see an English fish and chip shop on my travels. Is the world unaware of the joys of a piece of battered cod and a bag of soggy chips drowned in vinegar?

After just a few minutes of walking the streets I really warmed to the place. The people seem very friendly and polite in a reassuringly old-fashioned way (and I don't just mean that no one has called me a 'pommy bastard' yet). Charming manners is not the quality most Brits would think of associating with the Aussies, but anyone who troubles to find out a bit about other countries knows that these caricatures of nationalities are rarely accurate.

Once again there are lots of Japanese and Japanese restaurants. I suppose

Not the best place to put the sign, at the base of a coconut tree

we are in their backyard here in the Pacific, but the thought crosses my mind: are there any left in Japan itself? It's the same whenever I have been on holiday in Europe – I am always staggered by the number of Germans. Japan and Germany have two of the most successful economies in the world and yet they all seem to be on holiday the whole time. Who's doing all the bloody work? Or maybe that's the point: their economies are so efficient that they can afford to take more time off than the rest of us to enjoy the fruits of their labour.

We have barely had time to gather our belongings – let alone our thoughts – when the schedule demands that we take to the skies once again for our umpteenth flight. It's just as well I don't suffer from fear of flying or air sickness. At Cairns airport we were weighed because we were getting a small, private plane for the trip. Oops: I am afraid this luxury living is exacting a heavy price on my girth; I have put on nearly a stone. It seems that if the burgers don't get you first, then the French fries will.

LIZARD ISLAND LIES AT THE NORTHERN END OF THE GREAT BARRIER REEF, ABOUT 30 MILES off the mainland and 100 miles north of Cairns. It is only a short journey to the island, which is a luxury private resort owned by Qantas, the Australian airline. We have been told to prepare ourselves for a seriously beautiful tropical island and an equally luxurious hotel complex. I think I will be able to handle it.

The prospect of all this seems to have lifted the mood of the crew. We are all a bit tired after the recent travelling, the checking in and out of hotels, lugging bags and being processed through endless airports, but there was a distinct sense of excitement as we crammed into our tiny 10-seater. I am also starting to feel very excited about our scheduled dive in one of the most incredible sites in the world. I am told that the marine life is even more diverse and colourful than the Maldives where I dived about 10 or 12 years ago.

I will be amazed if the waters here are more impressive than those, which were absolutely teeming with hundreds of weird and wonderful fish, dolphins, turtles, any kind of sea life you can imagine. And I mean teeming: it was the marine equivalent of Piccadilly Circus in the rush hour. I don't know what it's like now, but the Maldives then were largely unspoilt and visited by only a handful of tourists, mainly because it was so expensive. But I wouldn't be surprised if it has now been inundated with visitors, probably to the cost of the local environment.

Nowadays, of course, you can leave work, go straight to the airport, pay 399 quid and wake up the next day in some paradise. The journey by boat from Britain to Australia for the first settlers used to take nine months and even the first direct flight, just after the First World War, took four weeks! The convenience of modern air travel has shrunk the world. That's a wonderful thing in that ordinary people are able to visit places that the previous generation could only dream or read about. On the downside, it also means that there are very few areas left in the world which you can genuinely call unspoilt. I can't think of anything worse than going to a remote part of the world to get away from it all and finding I'm next door to the family who live down the road at home. These paradises, of course, still exist, you just have to look a bit harder – or pay a bit more. We are buzzing towards one in our little plane as I write this and look down at the shimmering turquoise ocean below.

Lizard Island suddenly hoved into view as our pilot swung the plane around to land. It looks every bit as stunning as we had been led to expect: small, lush, mountainous and fringed with brilliantly white beaches. It was hard to believe that there was a runway anywhere down there but as we made our descent between two mountains we spotted a small strip of asphalt which looked no bigger than a stick of chewing gum. As the pilot throttled back and took aim at this terrifyingly small strip of flat land, I have to confess that I swallowed hard, bit my lower lip and hoped that I'd remembered to wear my reinforced underwear.

I am rarely frightened when flying but on this occasion I was aware that the pilot's margin for error was incredibly tight. At any normal airport the length of the runway gives the crew that much longer to bring the plane to a halt, but Lizard Island's 'runway' looked more like a helipad. There were 10 of us crammed into this tiny little plane with about 50 pieces of luggage wedged into the hold. Thermals (caused when the heat from the land meets the cool air off the sea) were creating a considerable amount of turbulence and as we began our descent we were being bounced around like ping-pong balls in a plastic bucket. There would be a lull as the plane was lifted by another blast of air and then we would drop alarmingly and find ourselves being lifted almost out of our seats. Somehow, though, we squeezed between the two mountainsides and it was with a great sense of relief that I felt the wheels make contact with Wrigley's landing strip. 'Gee, that was a bit hairy,' said our pilot. Just a bit.

We passed through the 'airport terminal' which is no more than a small wooden hut and – sing it to the heavens! – there are no officials, no passport control, no Customs officers, no policemen. We are met by some very friendly people who run this exclusive resort, where some of the world's top celebrities come to unwind. As we drive the short distance to the hotel I am amazed by the lushness of the island. Its peak is at 1,200 feet and boasts its own mini rainforest. It is a truly stunning setting for the hotel, where everybody has their own luxurious cabin set apart from the main building and tucked away in total privacy from your fellow visitors. It is quite the most wonderful looking hotel complex I have ever seen and it would be difficult to better it – even in your dreams. But you would certainly need a few bob to stay here from what I can understand ...

LIZARD ISLAND, SO CALLED BECAUSE IT IS HOME TO GIANT MONITOR LIZARDS WHICH can grow up to two yards long, is incredibly unspoilt. It is protected from development and abuse because the whole of the Great Barrier Reef has been turned into a National Park. Mercifully, there was not time for it to be ruined before the Australian government secured its protection. In fact, the biggest threat to the reef's future has come from nature itself. It has already been destroyed and created about 12 times as a result of changes in the sea-level. Coral can only grow at about 20 degrees centigrade, which means that a long-term fall or rise in sea-level will kill it off.

We learned all about Lizard Island and the Great Barrier Reef during one of the most delicious dinners I can remember having. Our wonderfully hospitable hosts gave us a run-down on the history of the reef and what we could expect to see when we made our dives. They also had a few words of warning about the potential hazards we should be aware of.

The Barrier Reef is about 1,200 miles long and 150 miles across at its widest. This gigantic structure was built by tiny creatures called coral polyps

The Lone Star Ranger toasts his starter

Sound asleep – Corky grabs forty winks

– an organism very low on the evolutionary ladder (I am resisting the temptation of making a joke about Ray at this point) – and consists of an intricate maze of islands and reefs with thousands of lanes and channels. The coral grows about two inches a year and most reefs take about 10,000 years to form. They are very fragile and divers have to take great care not to cause damage by standing or leaning on the coral as it dies once broken off.

There are 2,500 separate reefs in the chain where the warm waters are brimming with thousands of varieties of brightly coloured fish and other extraordinary marine creatures. Each reef alone can be home to up to 1,500 different species – more than can be found in the entire Atlantic Ocean. The Great Barrier Reef can still boast the highest concentration of marine life in the world despite the recent invasion of the coral-eating crown-of-thorns starfish which has denuded many areas. To give you some idea of its size and beauty, the white line of the reef is the only sign of life on earth visible from the moon.

The multicoloured coral sounds as if it is worth the trip alone, but it's the hundreds of exotic sea creatures I am most looking forward to seeing. The waters are full of parrot fish, moray eels (huge prehistoric looking creatures), the charming potato cod, lion fish, giant clams, scorpion fish, clown fish, sea anemones, giant grouper, squids, huge crabs, jellyfish, stone fish (a well-camouflaged, poisonous creature that sits on the reef bed), the dangerous blue-ringed octopus to name just some of the more 'glamorous' creatures.

Apparently we might also see some of the giant turtles I have heard so much about. I remember seeing a brilliant nature programme about these long-suffering creatures who emerge from the sea at night, like a scene from a sci-fi movie, to lay eggs in holes on the shore. It is an enormous effort for the turtles, which become very cumbersome on land. When the young ones are born they first have to dig themselves out of the sand and then make a 'dash' – at about one mile per hour – to the sea, avoiding the attentions of birds, crabs and other predators. Even then they are not safe. They have to keep coming to the surface of the water to breathe, but more often than not they are spotted by sea birds who pluck them out of the water for lunch. And even then, 50 per cent of those who have survived that far are killed by underwater predators on their way to deeper waters. Talk about a tough upbringing …

Simon, our diving guide while in Lizard Island, told us some cautionary tales about diving the reef. He reminded us that the clarity of the water and the beauty of the sights has been known to tempt divers to go deeper than they should, thus risking the 'narks', or nitrogen narcosis. The narks is a condition where a diver feels drunk or so elated that he loses his reason and becomes incapable of making sensible decisions (sounds a bit like most of the crew at 11 o'clock on a Friday night). He said he had seen divers under the influence of the 'narks' offering their regulators to passing fish! Simon knows that we are all very experienced divers, especially Ray, but it is good to be reminded of these dangers every now and then. Complacency or inattention under water can have terrible consequences.

We have already made two truly incredible dives on this trip, but I feel almost childishly excited about tomorrow's trip. It's like Christmas Eve and I cannot wait to open my presents. I went to bed in the best of spirits despite my back continuing to play up and being a little travel weary. This, for me, really is paradise – staying on a stunning, remote tropical island in a beautiful hotel with fabulous food and charming hosts, on the doorstep of one of the world's great natural wonders and one of its outstanding dive sites. My only complaint is that a certain lady at home is not here to enjoy it with me. Still, maybe another time ...

DAY SEVENTEEN

THE GREAT BARRIER REEF MAY LOOK BEAUTIFUL, BUT IT CAN BE A DANGEROUS environment for inhabitants and visitors alike. It is an underwater jungle where survival means eating or being eaten by your neighbours – or passers-by. They may look harmless but many of these creatures can seriously damage your health. Sharks, which certainly do not look harmless, are the biggest animal threat to humans in these waters. I like to think I am a fairly intrepid character but one of the scariest experiences of my life came during an encounter with these creatures during filming for a scene in the first series.

It was in Bermuda and we were taken down to do a scene where I would be filmed actually feeding the sharks. This guy normally goes out with a box of meat to feed them every couple of days, but these sharks hadn't been fed for a week because of the bad weather. When we arrived on the seabed, they were going absolutely mad. They were starving and we quickly found ourselves being bashed about by dozens of them, swarming all around us and tearing at the meat with row upon row of giant teeth. It was serious and for the whole time I was down there I thought my number was up. Back at the surface, I felt a bit like the returning fighter pilot who was one of the first to go in over the Falklands. While being debriefed he was asked, 'How did it feel?' to which he replied, 'I was scared fartless.'

No matter how many times you are reassured that everything will be just fine and that they will just eat the meat given to them, and no matter how brave and tough you think you are, when you see a giant set of teeth a few feet from your face, on the end of a powerful shark, you simply do not feel relaxed. The guy who took me down told me not to move my fingers from under my armpits or point because they would probably take my hands off. All the time I was thinking, 'What I do for the Great British Public, I must be off my head – they can go entertain themselves in future.' But like a good Brit I stood my ground, or more accurately, trod my water. The scene made stunning television and actually caused a bit of a sensation. After the programme we had lots of letters asking whether it had actually happened, whether it had been trick photography or whether we had used a stuntman in my place. I can assure you it was real – and I've still got the underpants to prove it.

On the boat on the way out, Simon, the dive leader, said the threat posed by the famous Australian sharks has been wildly exaggerated. There are about 300 varieties of shark in the world's oceans, of which only about 30 are genuinely dangerous to human beings. Hammerhead, white, blue and tiger sharks are the most dangerous, but they generally inhabit deep waters a long way from coasts. They are often found in harbours, like Sydney, because they have followed waste trails left by boats. Reefs, though, are never far from deep waters and immediately beyond the edge of them the depth of the ocean floor can plummet to about two kilometres.

Simon pointed out that the sharks that find their way into the Great Barrier Reef are extremely well fed. It's like a giant supermarket down there and by and large they won't bother you. If you go to a more remote reef where local sharks may never have seen a diver, they will approach more out of curiosity than with a view to lunch. But anyone who dives in tropical waters is told, if one does

Risking my life in the name of exciting television. Feeding the sharks in Bermuda

Pursuing a grey reef shark – one of the less dangerous varieties – at Half Mile Opening in the Great Barrier Reef

approach you and start bumping you around, you must stay calm. If you tense up or flap about the shark might attack. Being relaxed in these circumstances, as I discovered in Bermuda, is often easier said than done – especially when you know that sharks 'bump' their victims prior to attacking them. You never really know how a shark is going to behave, but it is a well-known fact that blood arouses their appetite and whips them into a mad frenzy.

For most of the trip out from Lizard Island there was very little talking. It's generally like that before a dive. Everyone is quiet and a little bit nervy; there is an air of apprehension. It could not be more different from the atmosphere when you get out of the water. Then everyone is suddenly incredibly talkative and even total strangers become extremely chatty. It's partly the exhilaration of what you have seen and partly the pumping adrenaline brought on by the relief that nothing went wrong and you are safely back on board.

As we reached our dive site the heavens opened and it began pouring down. I've never seen it rain so hard – not even in Manchester. They weren't so much sheets of rain as blocks of the stuff. We were getting soaked, not just from the rain but also from the spray as the waves hammered into the bow of the boat. We decided to kit up there and then and get in the sea right where we were as it was probably drier than staying on the boat! More importantly, time was now at a premium as the rain had delayed our departure and we were in danger of missing the giant clams we had come to find on our first dive. We slid into the warm, blue waters as the rain continued to pelt down above our heads.

Simon led us down on to the sandy bed in quite shallow water, but the visibility was very poor. It might as well have been back at Swanage, but maybe a degree or two warmer. Normally, you would be able to see a long way in these clear blue waters but the heavy rains during the night had stirred things up and we could only see about five metres ahead of us. We set off behind Simon, his bright green fins showing us the way as myself and Ray, carrying the camera, followed in tandem behind him. After about five or ten minutes of strong finning, we suddenly came across a coral reef and even though the visibility was still bad, it was a beautiful sight.

Reds, blues, greens and yellows created a great swaying kaleidoscope of colour and movement. In an instant I understood what all the fuss was about. No matter how well people describe it, you really have to see it first hand and at close range to appreciate the magic of it. There was something vaguely unreal about the vision before me and I wouldn't have been surprised to have seen a mermaid lying propped up on her elbow. It was also a real joy to see a reef that looked so vibrantly healthy. I've seen many in the past that had died and gone white – like the stuff you can buy on shore.

Thankfully these clams only eat plankton

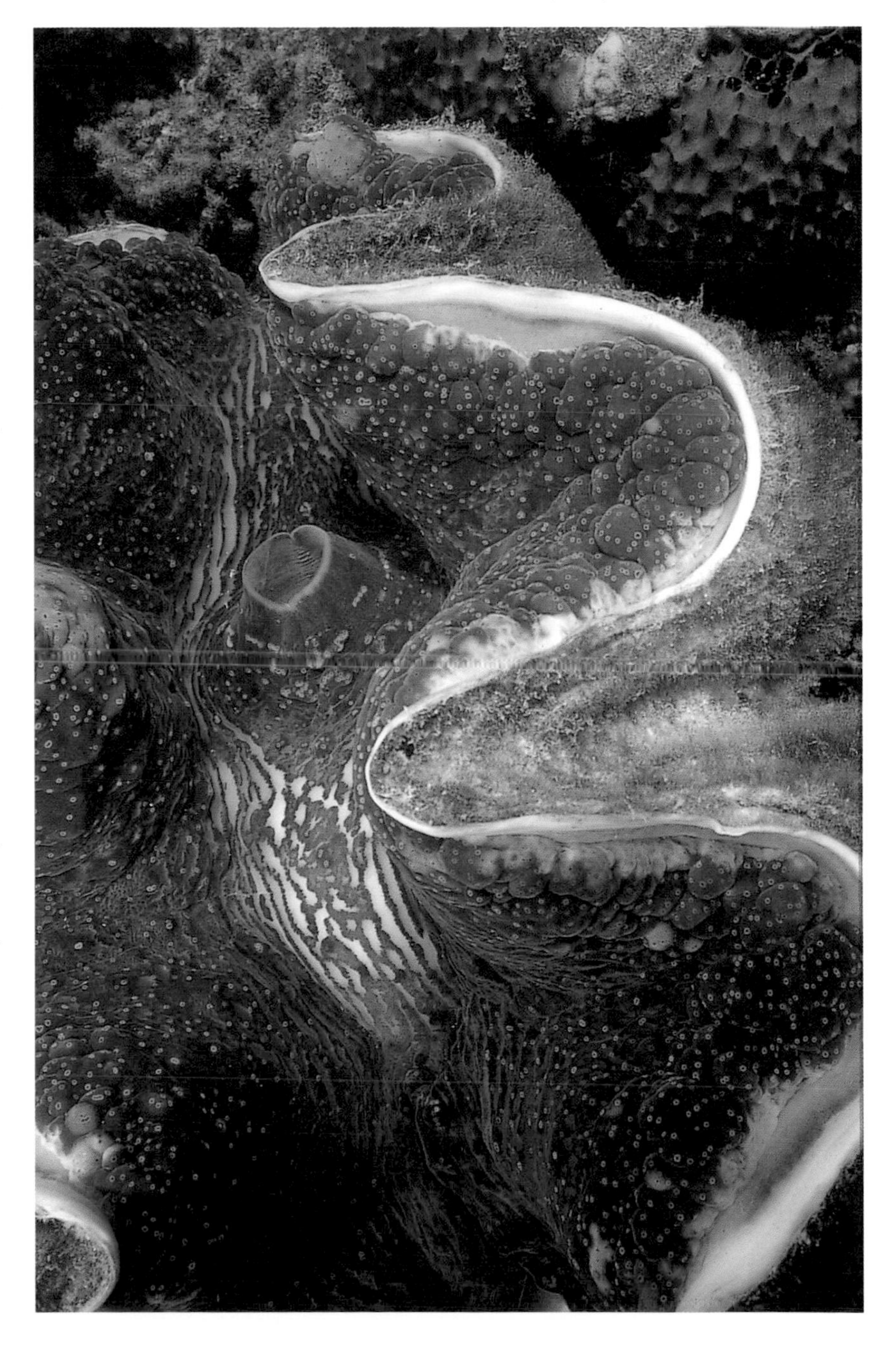

As we slowly finned our way through this stunning spectacle, leaving long trails of bubbles in our wake, we suddenly came across what we had set out to find – the giant clams. They are really impressive creatures and look exactly like the ones you see in the cartoons where the diver goes down wearing a big, round metal and glass diving helmet in search of shipwrecked treasure, only to be attacked by a huge octopus. After disentangling himself from the octopus the hero then treads on a giant clam which clamps its mouth round his foot and won't let go. These ones could fit a hell of a lot more than a foot inside them.

They must be about five feet by four. Far from being scary creatures they look vaguely

Any chance of a job on page 3?

Some people managed to stay out of the rain though – David Reynolds and Chanelle Garvey from the Lizard Island resort sit out the storm

Getting friendly with a starfish

comical while they sit there sucking water in and out, feeding themselves on the passing plankton. Just as cows and sheep stand around all day munching away on grass, so these creatures of the deep sit there grazing away on these microscopic animals that form the basis of the marine food chain. (Plankton are nature's unsung heroes – in addition to being a vital food source for invertebrates, fish and even whales, they also produce much of the earth's oxygen through photosynthesis.)

While the life of a plankter appears to be a pretty short one, these giant clams can live as long as 100 years so long as the water remains unpolluted. As I stared at these bizarre creatures, the extraordinary thought dawned on me that they may have been living on this reef since the Boer War. For all that time they have just sat there with their mouths open eating plankton. I hope they don't get restless or have long memories.

Unfortunately we had to tear ourselves away from this wonderful sight and head back to the boat for a surface interval before heading off for our second dive of the day. We are aiming for a famous dive site called Potato Cod Hole. It sounds a bit like an underground fish and chip shop cave to me, but apparently it is where dozens of these huge, peculiar fish live. The weather is still dreadful and the water is pretty rough as we set off south of the island. Slowed

This is what we had set out to find – the giant clam field

My new friend the potato cod

by the elements, our journey takes about an hour and the choppy waters prove too much for one or two members of the crew who became re-acquainted with their breakfast. Judy, our researcher, spent much of the trip down the reef leaning over the side, adding some natural colour of her own to the setting.

As we neared Potato Cod Hole the driving rain got even heavier and visibility above the water was as bad as it had been below. We are basically sitting in a dirty big cloud. We can't see the land, we can't see the sky, and we can barely even see the water a couple of metres beyond the boat. I remember the guy in the hotel last night describing the enormous complexity of all the lanes and channels in the Great Barrier Reef and the thought now crossed my mind that these conditions are probably about as difficult as they get in these parts. I began to hope and pray that the captain of our boat knows where he's going because we're buggered if we do!

Barely had these mildly unsettling thoughts had time to register when we suddenly found ourselves basking in glorious sunshine. Apparently these wild swings in the weather are common here at this time of the year. We arrived at a marker buoy and tied up to it as Simon briefed us about the dive and ran us through the do's and don'ts. (Don't put your head in the mouth of the potato cod, or prod the sharks, or kiss the jellyfish or sit on the poisonous stone fish – helpful little tips like that.)

The water was a bit clearer this time and soon after entering I found myself face to face with several large red fish with vicious teeth. They weren't smiling: they were hungry. We finned away from the boat with Simon carrying a box of fish to feed to the potato cod. We saw very little as we descended to a depth of about 30 feet but then suddenly, out of the gloom, appeared the star of the show. This is a seriously big fish: they can weigh up to 240 kilos and can grow up to six feet long and three foot wide. They were extremely friendly and inquisitive as they swam around us because they knew that Simon had got some food for them, just like a cat might rub itself up against your leg at dinner time. They may look stupid, but these potato cod know what side their bread is buttered – if you'll excuse this confusion of food images. They got so close to us that we were able to stroke and pat them as Simon handed out the goodies. He would hold out a piece of fish and it would disappear in a flash as the cod hoovered it out of his hand from about six inches away.

Swimming in the deep blue

News of this impromptu feast had clearly travelled fast and within a couple of minutes there were several of them circling us, giving us the friendly eyeball in the hope of getting in on the freebie. I had that same lovely sensation I experienced when we came across the manta rays in Hawaii; that wonderful feeling of being at one with nature and at peace with yourself. I felt entirely confident and safe amongst these bulky yet graceful creatures. Their wide open mouths and big staring eyes make them look endearingly thick. They are not what you would call beautiful, in the usual sense of the word, but their ugliness has a peculiar charm of its own. The water was lovely – warm, still and fairly clear – and it was an absolute joy to swim with these chummy creatures for half an hour, before the computers on our equipment told us it was time to return to the surface.

The potato cod seemed sad to see us go and they followed us all the way back to the boat. Before surfacing, I stopped off at a coral head where, just inside a crevice, there was a bright orange lion fish about 10 inches long. Simon had warned us that their beauty is deceptive and that they are, in fact, extremely poisonous. There is no real danger so long as you leave them alone

so we stared each other down for several moments as my potato cod escorts patiently waited for me to finish my nature-watch. I actually felt a little sad as I said goodbye to my new scaly friends and clambered back into the boat. Another wonderful dive. All the petty hassles and worries that inevitably arise on a long trip seem to sink to the ocean bed on dives like this. The buzz of the experience stays with you for the rest of the day but the memories, of course, will last a lot longer.

By now we were absolutely starving. You expend a lot of energy when diving – physical as well as nervous – and I had burnt up my breakfast long ago. (Other stomachs on board were empty for less edifying reasons.) The hotel had prepared us the most delicious picnic hamper for the trip, and as we headed back to land for a break in the diving we tucked into plates of fresh lobster, shrimp, salad, ham and bread rolls. I feel like a pampered celebrity at last!

WE HAD THREE MORE DIVES PLANNED FOR the day but the bad weather proved to be a major problem. It was very frustrating – after all, it's not every day you get the chance to dive the Great Barrier Reef. The dive in the morning had really whetted my appetite, but as the rain continued to hammer down in the afternoon we began to realize that the weather was going to wreck our plans. We tried one more dive but at the bottom of the anchor-line the visibility was only about 10 to 15 feet which is not great for diving and certainly not great for filming. We did not stay down long but there was just time enough to meet a huge stingray. All we saw at first was a pair of evil eyeballs glaring at us out of the sand and as we got closer this great creature rose up off the seabed and took off into the gloom. I hope we managed to get some good shots of it because it must have been about six feet wide, and it certainly cut a majestic sight as it reared up right in front of us.

It was wetter out of the water than in, as the heavens opened

A delicious lunch was had by all

The visibility deteriorated and a strong current was running so we were forced to resurface. The wind was really up now and the water was so choppy it was difficult to get back into the boat. We knew that was it for the day

MALIBU
DIVE
P·A·D·I
DIVEMASTER

and so we packed up our gear and headed back to Lizard Island. Everyone was clearly a little disappointed that we had been unable to complete the schedule as planned but there was obviously nothing we could do about it. On the way back, the captain of the boat told us that the highest peak on Lizard Island was the exact spot from where Captain Cook had finally plotted his route of the Barrier Reef. After several worrying months during which his ship almost sank when it ran aground on one of the reefs, Cook had scaled the steep hill and spotted an exit from this massive natural maze. Today the spot is known as Cook's Lookout.

DAY EIGHTEEN

I WAS ASKED TODAY WHAT I IMAGINED PARADISE TO BE LIKE. THE QUESTION WAS PUT to me as I sat nursing a freshly squeezed fruit cocktail and looking out over this balmy tropical landscape to the shimmering white sands and peacock blue sea. We had just finished the most exquisite lunch and had been talking about the incredible things we had seen in the reefs during yesterday's dive. Needless to say I did not have to scratch my head long to provide my answer. Lizard Island is exactly like those exotic settings you have seen in films of Robinson Crusoe. Very rarely does reality live up to fantasy, but here on Lizard Island I think it almost surpasses it. I am not going to gloat for much longer, but it would sound churlish and ungrateful if I recorded that this place was anything less than heavenly.

My turn behind the camera

The complex is entirely eco-friendly. All the rubbish that is produced is frozen and then flown back to the mainland to be disposed of there. Nothing stays on the island that wasn't there in the first place. And it is worth coming here for the food alone. It is all cooked by a Swiss chef called Fritz who has fresh produce flown in every day. When each course arrives at our table, always beautifully presented and just the right amount, the noise from our crew turns into a chorus of appreciation.

For lunch we had squid with tomato and basil on a sort of Chinese leaf base and it was without question the finest squid that I've ever had. It wasn't the normal rubber that you chew on for 10 minutes and then discreetly slip into your serviette and drop under the table. It just melted in the mouth. The fish, as you might imagine, is also fantastic and last night was the first time since I've been away that I've had some potatoes which actually tasted of potatoes. Even if the supplies from the mainland were cut off for some reason, I am sure you could still eat like a king, with all the fish and shellfish in the reefs and all the fruit and vegetables growing on the island.

I saw my first monitor lizard, which I am happy to say is not one of the delicacies on the menu – although I'm sure Fritz could find some way of making these prehistoric creatures look and taste delicious. I came across it as I was walking down the hotel path and saw it digging a hole in the ground. It was about four foot long and looked pretty severe, but apparently they pose absolutely no danger to humans. They are incredibly versatile creatures who can run fast, climb trees, catch fish in the lagoon and burrow deep underground.

I stood there and watched it for quite a while and it seemed quite undisturbed by my presence. Later on I saw some giant fruit bats which start to appear as the light fades and I felt very fortunate to witness all these lovely creatures in the wild. I have seen so many weird and wonderful creatures on our trip but I suppose they are only weird and wonderful because they are not familiar sights to us. Maybe if the locals came to Britain and saw foxes, badgers, deer, hedgehogs and other wildlife indigenous to our islands they would be filled with exactly the same sense of wonder that we are here. I suppose 'exotic' is no more than what you don't know or what you are not familiar with. For the inhabitants of a tropical island, a trip to the wilderness of the Yorkshire Moors or the Scottish Highlands or the gentle, rolling hills of Gloucestershire or Devon would be just as much of a thrill and an eye-opener. Well, I like to think so anyway.

DAY NINETEEN

I AM BACK IN MY HOTEL ROOM IN CAIRNS AND LITTLE HAS CHANGED. IT IS POURING with rain and my suitcases are still bursting at the buckles with dirty clothes. The situation has become critical. It is time to wash and boldly go. I've got one change of clean clothes and after that I either finish the trip naked or smelling to high heaven. The problem has been that we have barely stayed in the same hotel long enough to get our laundry done, and even when we have, we are generally rushing around to make sure the filming is completed. But we will be here in Cairns for a few days and the time has come for decisive action.

I now know where the expression ‘it never rains but it pours’ comes from – Cairns. Today you can’t see the mountains in the distance through the grey blankets of rain and mist that have enveloped the town. Apparently, the rain across Australia has been so heavy that there have been serious floods. Here in Cairns they’ve had a year’s rain in three months.

Drought, not flooding, is normally the biggest problem for Australia. It is the world’s hottest and driest continent and 70 per cent of it is either arid or semi-arid. There are no major rivers outside the eastern third of the country. Most of the lakes and rivers that you see on the maps exist only after a major rainfall and often they remain dry for several years. Not at the moment, though. The country is positively awash and judging by the pictures we have seen on the news, the floods look pretty disastrous in some parts.

Unfortunately, we are unable to reach one of our locations because it has been cut off by flood water and we have had to cancel the shoot. We are forced to continue on the hoof so Ray has gone off to try and find a dive operation which will brave the appalling conditions and take him out so that we can get some more underwater shots of the Barrier Reef. The rest of us head off to the rainforest in the mountains surrounding Cairns (where better to go when it is pouring with rain than a rainforest?).

Essential protection on the beach against the deadly box jellyfish

We travelled there by an incredibly long cable car ride which carries visitors about 5,000 feet up the steep mountainside. The construction of this cable car a few years ago became a major controversy in Australia and a *cause célèbre* for the environmentalists. The eco-warriors protested that in order to build the cable car the developers would have to destroy a great swathe of the forest to lay a road for the transport of building materials. Many of the protesters camped in the forests (I hope that they had some good insect repellent) and tied themselves to trees.

Most of them were slowly cleared but the last protester became a well known figure throughout the country after refusing to come down from his tree – the Australian Swampy. When police finally tricked him into giving up, there was a national outcry. Officers had dressed up as a film crew, equipped with cameras and microphones, and when the poor chap came down from his nest to tell the world about his protest, he was put in handcuffs and led away.

The weather continues to play havoc with our schedule

The protest, though, was successful in that it forced the developers into huge concessions. No road was built in the end and the giant pylons used to

The Cairns Post
Carry the TORCH
BUDGET Tourism Brochures
An Elle of a lure
BIGGEST WET IN 22 YEARS
FAR NORTH BUSINESSES GET EXPORT BOOST: PAGE 5
JULIAN
Bargain Buys
$119 pw
IMPREZA GX SEDAN
SAVE $1655
DRIVEAWAY
FANTASTIC FINANCE
SUBARU
GARFIELD
HEY CAT, WHAT DIDJA GET ON YOUR PIZZA?
BURRRP

On the web – a rainforest inhabitant poses for Denis's camera

carry the cable car up the mountainside were lowered into place by a fleet of Russian helicopters. Teams of construction workers on the ground had to enter the rainforest on foot in order to help the pylons into position. The protest had also forced the developers to guarantee that every single plant removed during construction work would be labelled and then replanted after the work was finished. It was a bitter struggle but ultimately most people were happy with the compromise. The cable car, an incredible sight and engineering feat in itself, was completed and not a single plant or tree of the rainforest was lost.

The views from the car, despite the rain and clouds, were absolutely stunning as we edged our way up over the Aboriginal land at the foot of the mountain and through the lower reaches of the rainforest. Myself and half the crew got out at the half-way point to meet our Aboriginal guide while the rest of the team continued to the summit.

I suppose I could lie but I can't – I couldn't get out of that bloody forest quick enough. Let me say from the outset that I yield to no one in my determination to see that the world's rainforests are preserved. It is terrible that so many millions of square miles of it around the world have already been destroyed by greedy developers, foresters, farmers and even governments. The rainforests are the land equivalent of coral reefs, home to thousands and thousands of life-forms. These forests must be protected, but as far as I am concerned they must also never be entered.

Today we ventured no more than about 100 yards into this steaming, dense, humid, moist, dark, noisy world – and that was quite far enough

My guide, Milton, and I scour the rainforest for the mozzie that just took a piece of my arm

Jim filming above the rainforest canopy. I'm out of picture, furiously scratching myself

A male and female peppermint stick insect get intimate

frankly. Within 10 minutes I was scratching myself like a flea-ridden dog with a bad case of eczema. Mosquitoes, ants, leeches, centipedes and any other hideous species of insect you can think of obviously saw me getting off the plane at Cairns airport. There were insects dropping on to me from trees, crawling up my legs, buzzing in my ears, burrowing in my hair and biting parts of my body that not even a glass of Heineken could reach. There were evil-looking snakes and giant hairy spiders. Even the plants joined in the fun, wrapping their barbs and branches around us. I felt like I was living out some kind of nightmare. I love nature but I don't want to be eaten by it.

I returned to the hotel cursing and scratching and muttering dark thoughts about the insect world. Back in my room I plastered myself from head to foot in anti-insect ointments and sprays. My entire body was covered in dozens of lumps and bumps and to make matters worse, my back is killing me again. I saw another chiropractor this morning who told me that I should apply ice packs to my back as often as possible. He also gave me a new course of medication and pain killers. And I've got a cold. I feel like a bloody mobile chemist, rattling with pills and covered in every brand of lotion you can think of. My mood was not improved when I looked out of the window. It was not even six o'clock but the rain was lashing so hard and the grim, grey clouds were so low that it was almost dark. The stormy weather just about sums up my mood right now.

I cheered up later, though, when Jim the cameraman told me about an amusing experience he had had earlier in the day. There was a couple of hours' gap in the schedule so he decided to go and relax by the pool. There was not a cloud in the sky, so he pulled up a sun-lounger and put his head down for a cat nap. He woke up slowly dreaming that he was in a lovely warm shower. It took him about five minutes to realize that he was in fact lying under a great tropical storm. He was absolutely soaking as were all his possessions and there was not a trace of the dozens of other sunbathers who'd been there when he arrived.

DAY TWENTY

GUESS WHERE WE WENT TODAY ... AN INSECT FARM! I THOUGHT THAT IT WAS SOME KIND of bad joke when I was told last night where we would be going. It actually turned out to be a really interesting and bite-free day. The journey there took us through some spectacular countryside and it was great to see the rainforest – in the distance and from inside the truck! The insect sanctuary was run by three characters called Jack, Sue and Paul who showed us dozens of extraordinary creatures – in a controlled environment. We saw praying mantises and giant cockroaches as well as a number of poisonous and hairy spiders. In the rainforest environment you get what scientists call 'gigantism' and many of these insects were seriously big. There were also some beautiful butterflies and moths which started life as caterpillars in jars. Some of these

A Hercules moth caterpillar at the insect farm, Garradunga, Queensland

caterpillars can take up to two years before they mature into butterflies, which is maybe nature's way of ensuring that, in the event of a bad year, there would always be some butterflies in reserve.

The owners of this fascinating farm, which is spread over 50 acres, have done an incredible job. The area used to be open farmland but in the space of about 50 years their family has managed to restore the dense forest that used to grow here before the European settlers arrived with their cattle. It was reassuring to see how nature had grown back so quickly and so vigorously.

The evening was to end with a few red faces and slapped wrists after a couple of members of the crew got a little carried away in the hotel bar and decided to do a bit of extra-curricular filming. David, Anton, Mike and myself decided to go out for dinner in town. When we left there was a private party going on in the bar, made up mainly of some brassy looking tour operators. On our way back into the hotel at about 10.30 we noticed that the party had grown considerably in size and noise. Right at the epicentre of the fun we saw three members of our crew. (The guilty parties shall remain nameless, apart from Ray.) It turned out that the guys were making an impromptu film about our diving guru, to be called 'Ray Williams In His Element' and featuring a series of interviews with some of the local tour operators. A few beers had clearly been drunk and, needless to say, the chief executive was not overly impressed to find his staff working on this spontaneous comic masterpiece. The tape of the proceedings was confiscated, a few harsh words were delivered and apologies were muttered before everyone shuffled off to bed. Whoops.

Are you looking at my pint? Exchanging pleasantries with Dave Aggis, the landlord of the Garradunga Hotel. We popped into this local hostelry after our visit to the insect farm

DAY TWENTY-ONE

Things to do, and not to do, on the beach at Cairns

TODAY WAS OUR SCHEDULED DAY OFF SO I WENT SHOPPING AND EXPLORED A BIT more of Cairns. There seems to be a fair number of British people here, which I hadn't really noticed before, and as I wandered around town even a lot of the locals seemed to recognize me. Apparently *The Darling Buds of May* was really popular here.

There is little to report today as we spent most of it relaxing, reading, making a few telephone calls home and catching up on some sleep. But I am happy to report another comic episode involving the inimitable and trouble-prone Ray Williams. The Australian two-dollar piece, which is worth nearly a pound, is the size of a British five-pence piece. Thinking they were virtually worthless, Ray had amassed a bulging pocketful of these and when it came to tipping the waitress at dinner he dumped a whole handful of them on to the table as we left, assuming that it amounted to a few dollars. The waitress had whisked away the pile of coins before it was pointed out to him that he had left her about £30!

Welcome to Australia

CAIRNS
CITY COUNCIL
CAIRNS CITY COUNCIL
Visitors and Residents are required to observe the restrictions depicted below. Co-operation will prevent the need for prosecution.

EXCEPT ON LEASH :-
-BEFORE 9AM
-AFTER 5PM
DAILY
ADVISORY SIGNS

CAUTION
NOV-MAY

NOV-MAY
STINGER RESISTANT ENCLOSURE

CHIEF EXECUTIVE OFFICER
SUN SMART
Save your skin
SPF 15+
CITY OF CAIRNS
QUEENSLAND CANCER FUND
QUEENSLAND HEALTH

DAY TWENTY-TWO

TODAY WE WENT TO FILM A LADY CALLED DI WHO RUNS A WILDLIFE RESCUE HOSPITAL with her husband just outside Cairns. People bring in wallabies, kangaroos, birds and other creatures that have been wounded in the wild. One of the animals was a 'wallaroo' which looks like a small kangaroo. I presumed it was a cross between a wallaby and a kangaroo but, in fact, it is a separate species altogether. Orphan baby wallaroos are called 'pinkies' because they don't have any fur, just pink skin, for about the first three months of their lives.

When someone brings in a pinkie, Di plays the surrogate mother, pops it in a little pouch and tries to keep it at a certain temperature. The main difficulty is that they have to be fed every two hours with special lactose-free milk. Now, some people may not want to know this but when a little pinkie has been fed, a wallaroo mother makes her baby go to the toilet by licking its bum. I should make it clear that Di and her colleagues do not have to replicate this process, but they do get up every two hours to feed the pinkie and then tickle its bum a lot with tissue to encourage it to go to the toilet. They really are incredibly dedicated people.

The main aim of the sanctuary is to help the wild animals recover and then return them to the wild. This can be quite a complicated and painstaking process as most of the animals quickly become dependent on the carers, especially if they are young. So they slowly wean them off their carer by giving them to another person before putting them into a cage and then finally releasing them back into their natural habitat.

It was a very rewarding trip and I was left with a great feeling of admiration for all the selfless people who work there. You hear so many tales of woe about what man has been doing to the environment that I find it very reassuring when you meet these characters just quietly going about the business of trying to make the natural world a better place.

Diana Mavjean and one of her hand-reared orphans at the North Queensland Wildlife Rescue

Elizabeth, one of the hand-reared wallaroos

Pepe, an orphaned walleroo with a dodgy hip

Feeding a pair of orphaned flying foxes (opposite, top)

A common bush tail possum gets in the hair of John Lee, one of the animal rescuers (opposite, bottom left)

Getting to grips with a black-headed python at the rescue centre (opposite, bottom right)

After a now traditional lunch of burger and chips in an anonymous roadside burger joint, we head for the airport to make yet another flight. By the time this trip is over I will probably have spent as much time in the air and under water as I have spent on the ground. I suppose that makes me some kind of rare species of flying amphibian. This flight turned out to be one of the more eventful of our expedition. Although I wouldn't go so far as to say that my whole life flashed before me, we certainly got as far as the trailers.

We were travelling in two planes, one for the crew and one for our equipment, and as we approached Airlie, our next shooting location, all I could see ahead was this huge wall of pitch black cloud. Feeling a little nervous about the prospect of flying straight into the eye of what looked like Hurricane Genghis Khan, I brought up the subject with the pilot. He assured me that we'd be landing in a few minutes so there wasn't a problem. He sounded very cool – but that's exactly how pilots are meant to sound.

I love it when you are on a commercial flight in a big jet and you hit bad turbulence and the plane starts crashing up and down and a few people start yelping and the children start crying; then the captain comes on over the intercom and starts talking so smoothly and calmly that you would think he was just cruising around a cocktail party: 'Hello, ladies and gentlemen, I hope you are enjoying the flight. We are currently travelling at about 30,000 feet about 1,000 miles off the Canadian coast and we are on course to land in about two and a half hours. Some of you may have noticed that we are experiencing a little turbulence at the moment, but we should be through it in the next 15 minutes. In the meantime, I hope you are enjoying the in-flight

An electrical storm brought amazing colours to the sky as we landed on the deserted airstrip

Sitting comfortably? At the controls of our plane to Airlie Beach

film and your soup…' And then you hear a snort of laughter before the intercom is switched off.

Our pilot today had just the same unflappable manner: 'No worries, mate.' A few moments later I suddenly saw an almighty flash of lightning and it started to rain so heavily that the plane seemed under water. There was no getting away from it – we were heading straight into this dirty great tropical storm. The crew went very quiet and as we got nearer the thunder boomed and cracked and the lightning flashed and forked. When the landing field suddenly came into view it was a huge relief. The pilot, keeping the plane steady in the unstable atmosphere, did a tight circuit and landed beautifully in what seemed the absolute middle of nowhere – not another human being to be seen. We managed to get our equipment into the van before the rain hit us with another deluge, and as we drove towards the town centre it stopped just as suddenly as it had started.

Airlie is like a mini-version of Blackpool – lots of lights, lots of bars and full of natives rather than foreigners. Our hotel was extremely basic compared to the luxurious ones we had been lucky enough to be staying in so far. In fact, it was so basic that both the bar and the restaurant were closed for restoration. It was like a big boarding house in Margate. We just had time to grab a quick shower and a bite to eat. I have to say that my first impressions of this town were not that positive and I do not think I will be rushing back for my annual holiday next year. The following will give you some idea of the kind of place we were in.

On the way back from dinner we passed a bar with some kind of act on stage. The comedian – I use the term in the loosest possible sense – said: 'There's a lady down the front here with a big pair o' bazookas. I reckon she oughta take her shirt off and show us, what do you think?' The crowd roared, 'Yeah, let's see her bazookas.' Ho ho. I think you get the picture.

DAY TWENTY-THREE

TODAY WE MET ROB, A FORMER BUSHMAN WHO IS AN EXPERT ON AUSTRALIAN WILDLIFE. Rob manages a wildlife park which contains emus, ostriches, flying foxes, crocodiles, snakes, spiders – name your creature and Rob will probably have it wrapped around his neck, running up his sleeve, sitting on his shoulder or tugging at his leg. He was kind of a cross between Crocodile Dundee and St Francis of Assisi. He took us to the snake pen which contained some of the most poisonous snakes in Australia. Oh great, I thought, another scene where muggins has to frolic with some of the most dangerous creatures in the world for the amusement of the Great British Public! He wanted me to join him in there, but I cordially declined his kind invitation and stayed by the safety of the door.

Rob Bredl, the 'Barefoot Bushman'

While he was talking to camera about his snakes, I noticed a green box at my feet which I thought contained electrical equipment. Rob then casually sauntered over and lifted the lid of this box. It was seething with dozens of snakes, some of which made a dash towards me. I will do virtually anything – within the bounds of good taste and standards – to entertain an audience, but messing around with dangerous reptiles is one act that I prefer to leave to the experts. These were some of the deadliest snakes in the world and Rob was letting them slither all over him! He said that he was not frightened because he had managed to tame them and win their trust.

He particularly wanted to show me a taipan, the most poisonous snake in the world. When he went and fetched it out of its cage I can tell you that the entire crew, as one man, took four paces backwards. I was left

Rob insists on showing me a taipan, the most poisonous snake in the world. Note how I bravely stood my ground.

there with this killer staring at me, four inches from my face, while Rob cheerfully told me that if it decided to bite and hit a vein I would have just three more seconds of my life to enjoy. If it missed the vein, I would have a few minutes longer. (It's reassuring to know that the snake has a such a sporting side to its nature.) Well, I am proud to report that I stood my ground in true British fashion, although I drew the line at letting this evil-looking beast writhe all over me.

That, you might have thought, would be enough brushes with death for one day, but Rob was not done yet: I hadn't met his friend Solomon – a 17-foot crocodile. Rob cordially invited me into Solomon's house and before I knew it I was standing a few feet from this terrifying beast with a bucket of chicken pieces. I foolishly rattled the bucket and Solomon took a lunge towards it. I saw the crew on the other side of the enclosure grinning, half nervously, half sympathetically (I think).

Crocodiles are living dinosaurs that have been terrorizing their habitats for millions of years – one of the few creatures to survive the Ice Age. They've got very, very small brains but immensely powerful jaws. Joe, Rob's brother and the owner of the park, told me a blood-curdling story about his daughter Carla and Solomon. A year or so ago, Carla, who had grown up with and worked with these creatures all her life, slipped and fell in the cage when she was feeding Solomon for the benefit of some tourists. As she fell, Solomon snapped his jaws on to her upper thigh and dragged her into his pool. (Crocodiles often kill their prey and then store them under water until they are hungry.) Joe heard her screams and came running. He leapt in over the

My second brush with death in one day, as Solomon lurches forward to grab a quick lunch

A saltwater crocodile, no doubt thinking, 'Where's that tasty-looking David Jason fellow?'

Carla Bredl with her dad Joe – and Solomon who almost killed her (opposite)

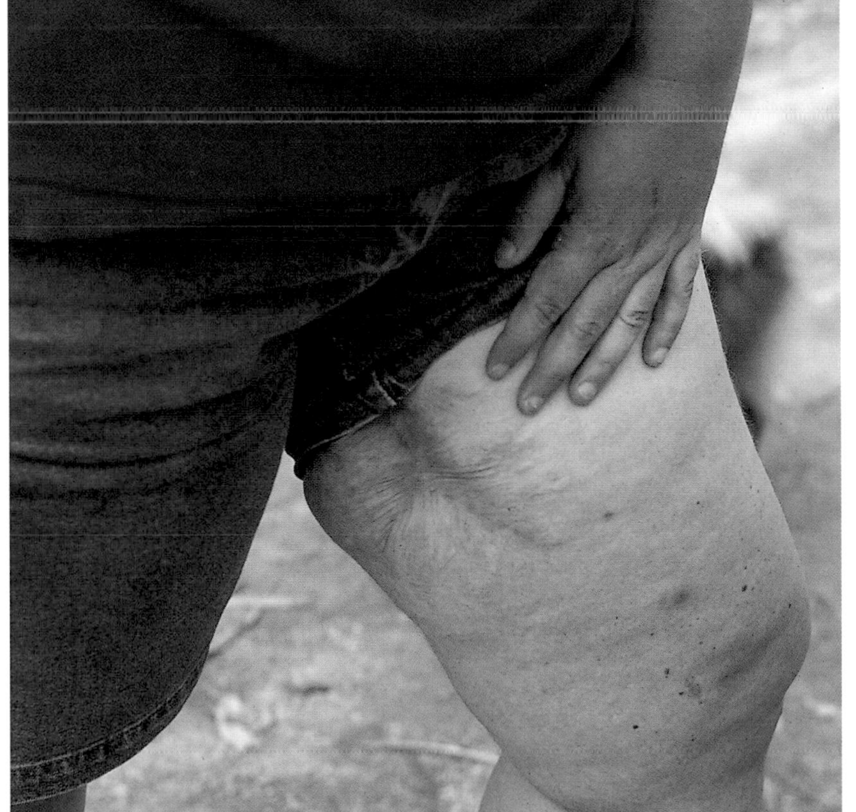

Carla shows one of the scars from her terrifying crocodile attack

Anton and I get a helping hand from our furry friend

gate and jumped on the back of the crocodile, which instantly let the girl go. But Joe lost his grip and the crocodile took another snap at Carla, breaking her pelvis in two and gashing open her stomach and her upper torso. Solomon dragged Carla under the water again and, as a last desperate measure, Joe jumped on its back again and began to gouge its eyes. It worked; Solomon opened his jaws and let go of Carla before sinking to the bottom of the pond. Other rangers had arrived on the scene and with the help of some of the public, they dragged Carla out of the enclosure while Joe managed to jump out of the pool away from the danger.

Carla was rushed to hospital and her injuries were so severe that the specialists had no idea where to start. Incredibly, she lived – even though she has undergone a total of 31 operations since that terrible day. Even more incredibly, she's back here working with the crocodiles. She's an unbelievably jolly girl considering her horrific experience. I asked her if she thought Solomon should have been shot and she said 'Not at all', because it was her fault not his. What an amazingly tough and positive family.

As you can imagine, by this stage I had had just about enough of the reptile kingdom and I needed little persuading to go and meet the koala bears. They are every bit as lovely as you might think and it was wonderful to be able to hug and play with them. But you wouldn't want to get on the wrong side of one in the wild. Their claws are like razors and when they feel frightened they can use them to vicious effect. The female of the species is much prettier than the male. The one that I was holding kept nibbling my ear with

In pole position: a koala prays he isn't mistaken for Corky's boom

its sharp little teeth but the trainer promised that she wouldn't do a Mike Tyson and take a lump out!

It has been another fascinating day – if a little heart-stopping at times – but there is little chance for us to reflect on it because our circus is on the move to the next town. We headed back to Cairns on our little aircraft and this time there were no storms, thank heavens – I've had enough excitement today to last me a year. We were all exhausted after another long day and most of us fell asleep before arriving at Cairns.

A man of many talents: David Reynolds, executive producer . . . and boom operative

DAY TWENTY-FOUR

THERE WAS NO CHANCE OF A LIE-IN THIS MORNING BECAUSE WE ARE OFF TO FILM AT the famous gold fields in the middle of the Australian bush – or 'The Great F*** All' as they affectionately call it here. We assemble for breakfast at seven o'clock where as usual I am given a run-through of the plans for the day's shoot: where we are going, who we are going to meet and what we are going to do. Like good boy scouts, we are always well prepared.

We fly by helicopter, which I absolutely love. It is such an exhilarating way to travel. For a start you are sitting in what seems like a huge armchair compared to the seats you are given on airplanes. From there you have more than 180 degrees of vision which gives you this incredible sensation when the helicopter suddenly pulls you into the air and you see the ground rapidly receding below you. It's the same pleasantly stomach-turning feeling you get on rides at a theme park.

We travel across the rainforest – how blissful to be above it and not in it – before heading deeper and deeper into the bush, which is every bit as arid and barren as I had been led to expect. There are unimaginable distances of orangey, scorched earth and rock as far as the eye can see. Virtually the only sign of life visible from the air are the thousands of termite mounds. Finally, we arrive at our destination – a tiny speck of civilization in the middle of this

Skippy and I take a break between shoots at the Airlie Beach Wildlife Park

Arriving by helicopter at the Tyre Connell Gold-mine in the middle of the Australian outback

giant wilderness. We circled above the gold-mine and I was convinced there was nowhere to land as we hovered over this rocky outcrop. But we began to descend and somehow the pilot found a space that we managed to squeeze into by a matter of inches – and I mean inches. Remember the strip of chewing gum on Lizard Island – well, this was more of a postage stamp. As we went down there was a giant eucalyptus tree no more than about a foot from the cockpit!

We had arrived in Thornborough, a town spread over 125 square miles but with a population of … four. We met two of the residents, a young couple called Kate and Andrew, who showed us around this desolate outpost. They explained that all the buildings were made out of corrugated iron because it was so easy to assemble and after severe storms easy to pick up and put back together again.

It seems almost impossible to believe now, as you survey this ghost town today, but in 1870, at the height of the Australian gold rush, there were 18,000 people living here. Once the news was out that the Australian outback was supposedly rich in gold, settlers from all over the world poured into the country, causing a huge boom in the population. Most of the fortune-hunters were from Europe but there were also thousands of Chinese and Americans. Only a few, though, were to make a fortune and the people who did best out of the rush were the shopkeepers – especially the whorehouse owners – who set up in towns like Thornborough to sell their goods to the diggers.

Kate had done a lot of historical research into her hometown and she told us the story of a certain Mr Mulligan, the man who found the gold in the hills and then founded the town. The government gave him the statutory £1,000 pounds that they paid to people who discovered gold. The government made the payments because they wanted to open up the outback and they also wanted gold for trading and to lay down in the country's reserves. When

Mulligan returned to Thornborough he was followed by thousands of other hopefuls and within a few years a whole community had been built complete with houses, hotels, bars, shops, brothels and banks. It normally takes decades, even centuries for a town to reach this size. It just makes you realize what man is capable of achieving when he is told there might be some gold in it for him.

The new arrivals also constructed a steam engine – the parts of which were made in Leeds – to drive the shaft on the main mine. In order to fuel it they used the local trees as there was no coal. The settlers soon deforested the entire area but fortunately a few of the trees have since grown back. By the end of the century the gold rush had virtually petered out and the population of the town began to dwindle as people headed to the cities in the east to find other work.

Kate and I tried our hand at panning for gold in the stream. She said the recent heavy rains increased the chances of finding some because it would have washed down the mountainside. She was just being kind and encouraging but after about five minutes of standing up to my knees in mud I actually found some! Kate was totally surprised and I got carried away even though it was just a few flakes. There wasn't enough there to buy a packet of fags, or pay even a fraction of the dry-cleaning bill for my muddied clothes. But I didn't care – I had panned for gold and I had actually found some! There were prob-

With Kate Harley and Andrew Bell in Thornborough

Kate shows me the cemetery at Thornborough

Kate Harley at the Tyre Connell Gold-mine

Panning for gold, as Denis captures the scene on film (opposite, top)

I'm sure there's gold here somewhere. The dog, however, thinks I'm mad (opposite, bottom)

ably some gold-diggers who panned for months and never found a jot.

Kate and Andrew plan to restore the mine and some of the old buildings and turn Thornborough into a tourist attraction. It's going to take a long time and a lot of money, but they are confident that there are thousands of Australians who would want to see a major part of their history brought to life. A lot of foreign visitors, looking for the old Australia they have read about in books, would also make the trip. I would – so long as I could come by helicopter! The couple already cater for a number of tourists who want to experience life in the bush. But after a couple of hours or so you begin to understand why people do not want to put down roots here. The heat is almost unbearable and there are about 1,000 snakes and 10,000 spiders for every human being. (One of the biggest dangers is posed by a little red spider who lives under the toilet seat!) As it stands there is not a great deal to do here apart from lie in a cold bath, drink cold beers and dodge the wildlife.

Who says I don't have the Midas touch?

Before leaving we were introduced to the other half of the Thornborough population. They are Vince and Helen, the mayor and mayoress of the town. (The election process was not a long drawn-out affair and apparently they did not need too many recounts before announcing the result to the good people of Thornborough who had packed into the main square.) Vince also looks for gold with a metal detector and he showed us a bowl of golden nuggets that he had found as deep as six feet under ground. There were about two dozen

Vince and Helen, the mayor and mayoress of Thornborough (pop. 4), show off their collection of gold nuggets

of them, some the size of marbles, making Vince a very rich man. I suppose there was little chance of being robbed out there as strangers in town are pretty easy to spot.

As we said goodbye to the two couples and boarded our helicopter, it was eerie to think that this near-deserted, tumbleweed town once bustled with life. As we took off I looked down at four people where once there were 18,000 and for a fleeting moment I imagined all their ghosts crowded into the square below and waving us off. Another weird and wonderful place.

ONCE BACK IN CAIRNS THERE WAS JUST TIME FOR A QUICK SHOWER, A COLD BEER, A late supper and another comic scene involving our loveable Welshman. Over the course of the trip, Ray and one or two other members of the crew had developed this habit of calling out 'mine' every time a pretty lady walked by and 'yours' if she was not so pretty. When we got out of the taxi at a local restaurant that had been recommended to us, someone asked who was going to pay. No sooner had the question been asked than a very attractive lady walked right in front of the car and Ray shouted 'mine'. We all said,'Oh, thanks very much Ray, that's very kind of you', and shot into the restaurant, leaving our accident-prone dive guru muttering dark Welsh curses on the pavement.

DAY TWENTY-FIVE

THESE EARLY MORNINGS ARE STARTING TO CATCH UP WITH ME. I WAS ALMOST sleepwalking as I shuffled down to breakfast. The plan today is to head out for another dive on the Barrier Reef where we are going to use a new underwater communication system. A microphone cable from the boat will be connected to our face masks so that we can talk to each other while diving. (Well, that's the theory anyway.) Unfortunately, the terrible weather is still with us and it is absolutely lashing down again.

Producer Mike Treen and cameraman Denis try to succeed where King Canute failed

We headed down to the jetty where we met our dive leader for the day, a Barrier Reef expert called Paddy who is an Australian of Irish origin. He told us that there was absolutely no chance of diving today as the sea is incredibly rough, with the waves around the reef reaching as high as three metres.

The mission is aborted and instead we head off to the next best thing to the Barrier Reef: a simulated Barrier Reef at the local aquarium. We were given permission to dive in the great big pools and tanks, but were not allowed to wear our fins as they can seriously damage the fish, whose reactions are not quite as sharp as their wild cousins'. I imagined that filming in an aquarium would be a major disappointment after experiencing the real thing. But it was a fantastic experience as all the fish were tame and very friendly. There were my old friends the potato cod, who were even more hospitable and playful than the ones I had swum with out near Lizard Island. Even the stingrays and sharks came and played with us and there were all sorts of fish I could not recognize. It was a truly magical experience and although we were in a controlled environment it was an extraordinary feeling to 'bond' with these creatures of the deep.

DAY TWENTY-SIX

THIS WAS OUR LAST NIGHT IN CAIRNS AND WE HAD OUR FIRST LITTLE 'UPSET' OF THIS leg of the trip. We had gone to this lovely Chinese restaurant where we were seated at a table next to a large party. At the end of the evening, one of the women in the group, who looked like she was on the wrong end of a few pints of the amber nectar, invited herself over to our table. She was talking to Jim and Ray, but she kept looking over in my direction. I thought 'Here we go, a drunk Brit who looks in danger of creating an embarrassing scene', so I made a hasty exit. In fact she turned out to be a local whose husband (poor bloke) was entertaining some friends from South Africa.

Dinner passed off without incident and the rest of the crew went back to the hotel bar for a nightcap when, who should walk in, but the crowd from the Chinese restaurant. They were clearly a little worse for wear and the barman refused to serve them. The woman got really loud and aggressive and started to call our team 'a bunch of pommie bastards'. To their credit, the crew just bit their lips and sat there in silence, refusing to get involved, while the barman turfed the party out under a hail of verbal abuse. There are always a few morons wherever you go. We've got some excellent ones of our own back in England.

A slice of life in Oz – the public bar at the Garradunga Hotel

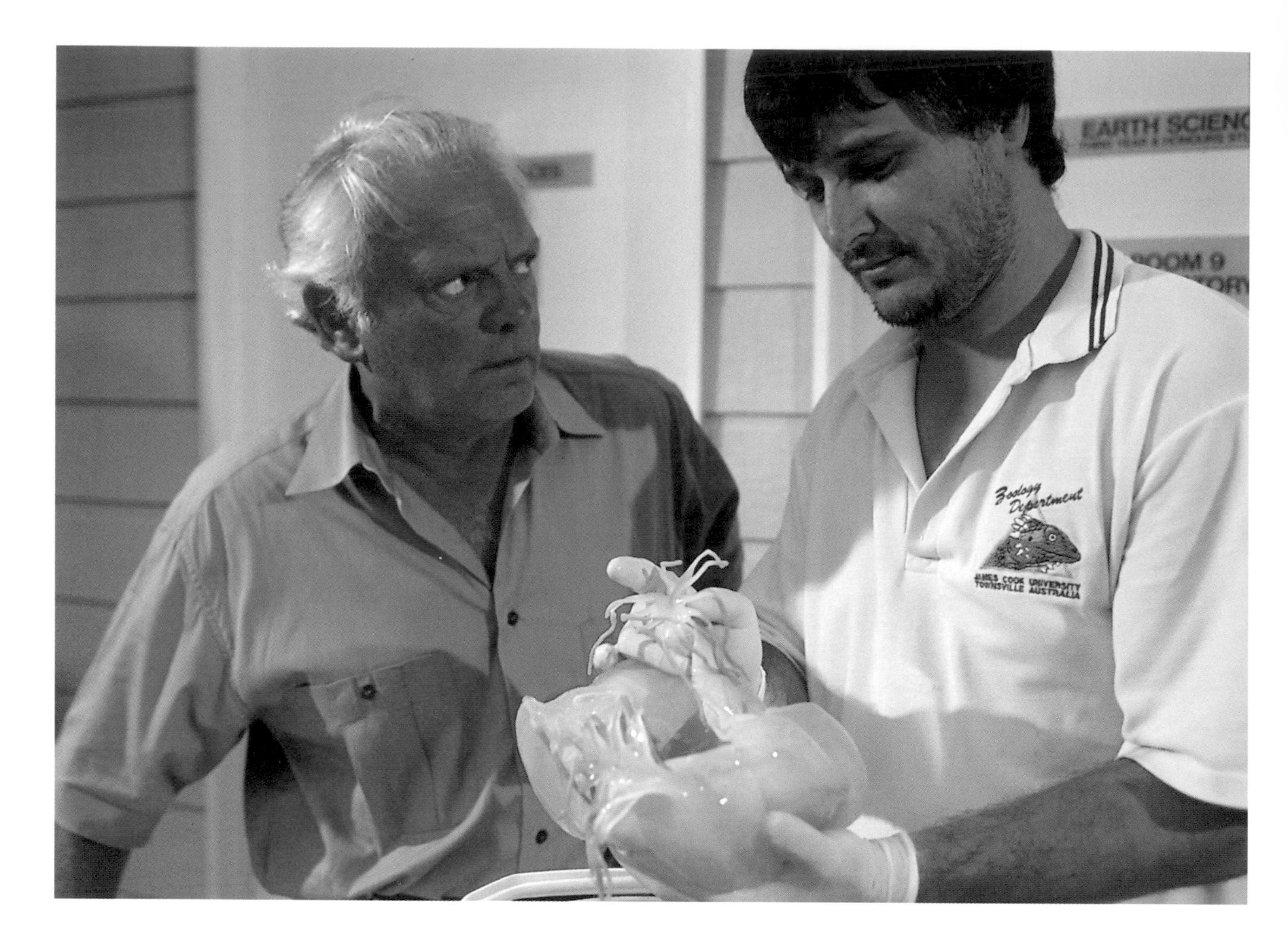

Jamie Seymour shows me a deadly box jellyfish at the James Cook University

DAY TWENTY-SEVEN

Today we went off to meet a vet called Peter Barrett to watch him treat another highly dangerous creature from the reptile world. This snake had a big lump in its gut which turned out to be an undigested rat! (It had obviously been to the same restaurant we went to just outside Cairns the other day.) During the interview he told us that more vets are injured and killed by domestic animals than by creatures they treat from the wild, including poisonous snakes. Horses, followed by cows, are the biggest killers.

Later we went to meet Jamie Seymour, a doctor of biology at the James Cook University. He is one of the world's leading experts on jellyfish. He told us about the different varieties of this alien-looking creature, including the box jellyfish. One type of box jellyfish is about the size of your hand and can give a very nasty sting that will lay you low for days. More extraordinary is its little brother which is no bigger than the nail on your little finger and has tiny tentacles (yes, the spelling is correct). Despite its size – you would have no chance of spotting it if you were swimming in the sea – it is seriously toxic and could kill you if it stung you on the chest. Apparently, they hang about in shallow water and people do not know at first that they have been stung. But a terrible pain hits you after about 20 minutes and if you don't get to hospital quickly you could suffer paralysis, nerve damage and even death. I found Dr Seymour's tales rather alarming and I will feel a touch nervous the next time I go skipping into the sea for a quick dip. Forget your tiger sharks, sea snakes and stone fish – at least you can see them coming.

Before going back to the hotel I paid another visit to the chiropractor for some more treatment, but there are only a couple more days of the trip to go and it doesn't look likely that my back problem is going to clear up. I am slightly dreading the long flight back as it was on the flight out here that the problem flared up in the first place. Maybe it will be a case of sod's law and as soon as I pass through Customs at Heathrow I'll feel as right as rain, but somehow I doubt it. (I found out later, from my chiropractor, Don Gatherer, that I had trapped the sciatic nerve. This is a serious problem, but thanks to his expertise I am back on track – if you'll excuse the pun – and on the road to recovery.)

I was told that we have shot over 40 hours of film since we started this project to make two one-hour programmes. It gives you some idea of the amount of work that goes into making a television programme, but it is just a shame that so much good material will inevitably end up on the cutting room floor. We've also flown 17 flights, although my wretched back could have told me that. You will be pleased to hear that I managed to do all my packing without uttering one nasty oath. This is mainly because my entire wardrobe is spanking clean and neatly folded after a final trip to the hotel laundry.

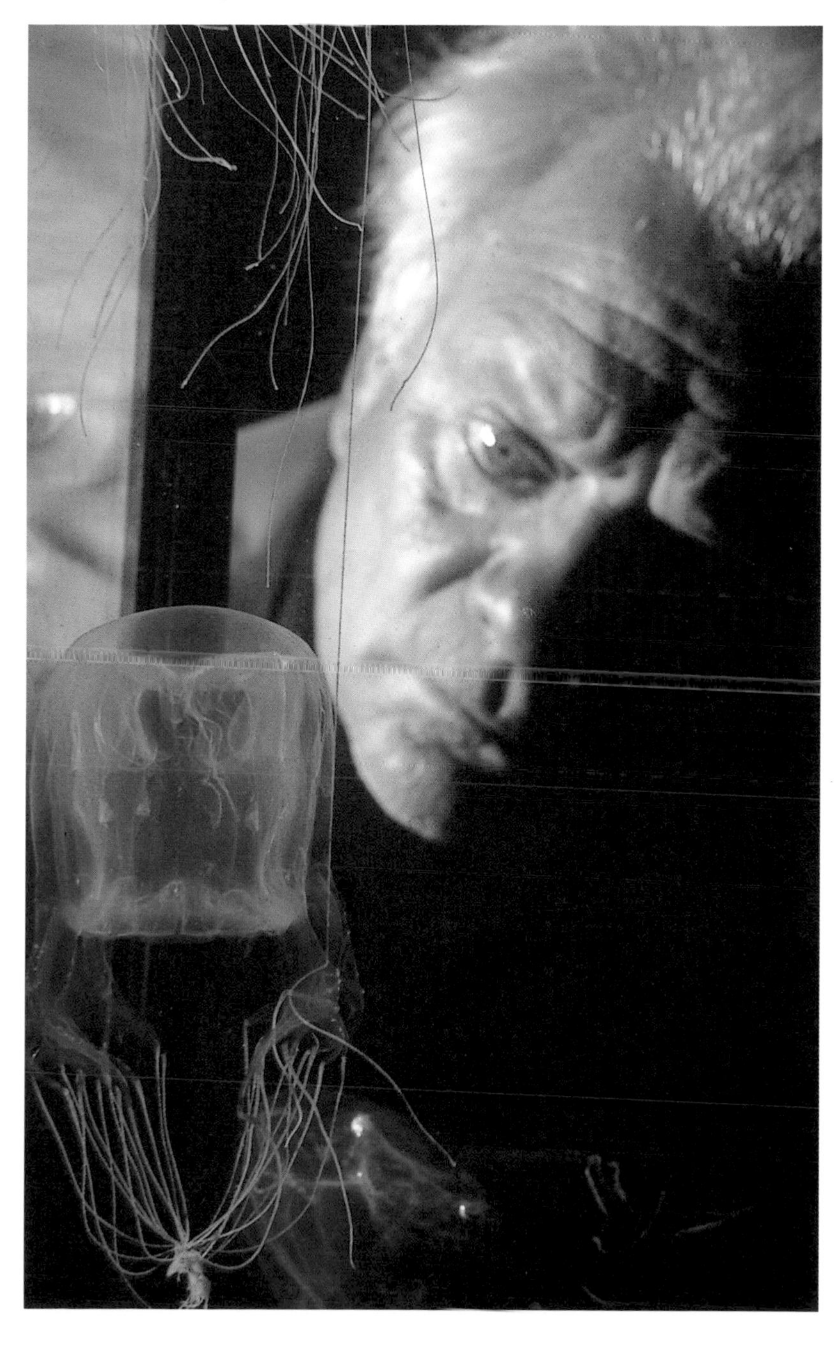

The box jellyfish (or sea wasp as it is also known)

DAY TWENTY-EIGHT

Today has been another 'travel' day and there is precious little to report unless you would like me to describe the inside of Cairns or Adelaide airport or the back of Ray's head which I spent five hours staring at as we headed to the final destination of our expedition.

The long flight to Adelaide from Cairns takes you from the north to the south of Australia and demonstrates just how massive this country is. We were in the air for over five hours, passing over thousands of miles of uninhabited, sun-scorched bush before touching down in the port capital of South Australia. The difference in the weather is another reminder of this continent's vastness. Whereas Cairns was hot and tropical, here the climate is more temperate. We arrived at the hotel at about eight o'clock and there was a distinct nip in the air. I actually found it quite refreshing after four weeks of mopping my brow and panting like an English sheep dog in the Sahara.

DAY TWENTY-NINE

For our final assignment we went to meet a man called Rodney Fox who runs a shark museum in Adelaide. He is quite a well-known figure in Australia, but not for reasons that he would have wanted. About 30 years ago, when he was in his early twenties, Rodney entered a spear-fishing competition on a beach not too far from where he now lives. He saw a large fish at about 25 feet and dived down to spear it. On his way back to the surface, with the blood trailing from his catch, he felt as if he had been hit by a No. 9 bus. He had just managed to recover his senses when he felt a tremendous pain – he had been 'bumped' by a great white shark and now he was in its jaws. Despite being in shock, he had the incredible presence of mind to stick his finger in the shark's eye and it promptly released him.

Rod just managed to reach the surface to take a breath of air and was about to shout to the other divers when he was attacked again. The great white dragged him under and started to spin him round. Once again he showed amazing initiative and fighting spirit, poking it in the eye once more. He managed to get back to the surface where, this time, he was able to raise the alarm. The water around him was red with his own blood and he could see the face of the giant shark coming towards him for another attack. This time it grabbed his arm but as it did so Rodney pushed his fist to the back of the beast's throat and it unlocked its jaws again.

The shark then turned and snapped hold of the large piece of bait attached to Rodney's weight belt by a rope and dragged him through the water at great speed. He said he thought he was seconds away from drowning but just as he was about to take a potentially fatal lungful of water, by some miracle the rope snapped and he shot back to the surface and began to shout for help. Again, by a stroke of sheer luck, a boat was nearby and he was dragged on board and raced to the shore.

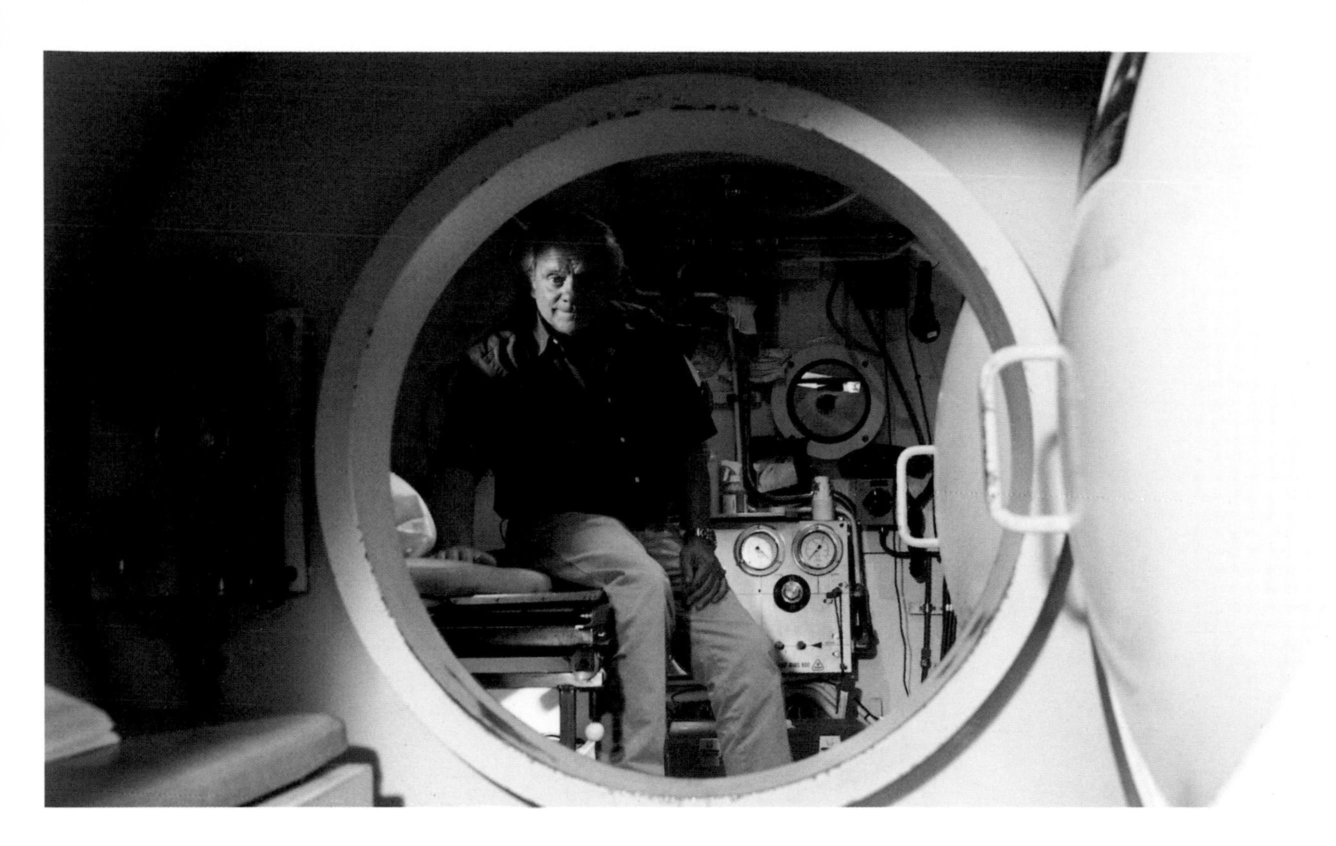

The recompression chamber at Royal Adelaide Hospital

He had horrific injuries all over his body but his rescuers drove a car right into the surf to get to him. The car got stuck but dozens of people helped push it back to land and he was whisked away to hospital. The journey took 40 minutes and the people in the car tried desperately to staunch the flow of blood. To give you some idea of the severity of his injuries, they had to push his intestines back in on the way. When they finally arrived at the hospital, the surgeons in accident and emergency said he had no chance of survival. He'd already lost most of his blood and his body had literally been torn to shreds. But the doctors went to work and for five days he remained on the critical list before he slowly recovered. Incredibly, he was to discover when he regained consciousness, the shark had bitten him just about everywhere but somehow hadn't pierced any of his main arteries. When they were adding the last few of several hundred stitches they had a bit of flesh that could not be sewn back on. When Rodney asked what they had done with it, the surgeon told him he'd fed it to the cat! (Or so the story goes.)

Before returning to the hotel we visited the recompression chamber at Royal Adelaide Hospital. This is where a diver suffering from 'the bends' is rushed. Some will emerge from it after five hours feeling absolutely fine, but others are not so lucky. If their ascent from the deep has been too rapid or they take too long getting to the chamber they can suffer brain damage or paralysis. Fortunately, I have never been inside one of these contraptions and I have only ever been involved in one incident where there was a 'bends' scare. It happened a few years back. There were about eight of us, including our platinum friend Ray, on a dive in the Caymans and one of the girls in the group had some kind of panic attack when we were about 60 feet down. You could tell she was in trouble because she had broken off from the rest of the group and started to become agitated. She was experiencing something

Lizard Island, the closest we came to paradise

called 'narrowing perception' – a condition brought on by panic when your vision becomes tunnelled.

Her instinct told her to get to the surface as soon as possible and she had tried to inflate her BCD (buoyancy control device). If we hadn't manage to stop her she would in all probability have died. I managed to hold on to her legs with one arm while I took my knife out with the other and banged it on my tank, which is the procedure to alert other divers of a problem. Ray heard the alarm and raced over. We both held on to her as Ray calmed her down and got her to breathe regularly. He was absolutely brilliant and almost certainly saved her life. Later, when the emergency was over and we were back on the boat, she couldn't explain what had happened, even though she was a very experienced diver. I think I can imagine what happened. Sometimes when you are diving you get this sudden and disturbing feeling that you are in a completely alien environment and that you are entirely at the mercy of your equipment. It is an awareness that you could die, I think.

TONIGHT WE PACK OUR SUITCASES FOR THE LAST TIME BEFORE GETTING ON OUR FINAL flight home via brief stopovers in Perth and Singapore. I have lost count of how many planes we have boarded but I think it must be at least 20, although it feels more like 200. We have crammed in so many unforgettable experiences over the last few weeks, it seems like months ago that we all first assembled at Heathrow. It has been a wonderful odyssey, and what I have seen, the experiences I've had and characters I've met will remain in my thoughts for a very long time.

Pearl Harbor, Randy the cowboy, the incredible hotels on Hawaii, the Japanese fleet in Chuuk Lagoon, the Great Barrier Reef, Lizard Island, that (bloody) rainforest, the helicopter ride over the vastness of the outback, the deserted gold-mining town, the animal sanctuaries and all the fascinating people and creatures that inhabit these places ... I have seen more on this one trip than the average person can reasonably expect to see in a lifetime and I feel very privileged to have been the given the opportunity to take part in this adventure.

One of the reasons why the trip has been so successful and enjoyable is the quality of the crew. To a man (and a woman in the case of Judy the researcher), everyone has been extremely professional and efficient, which makes such a difference. There have been a few minor cock-ups but the whole crew can feel very proud of their contribution to what I hope will make some stunning television. There has barely been a cross word spoken and we have had some highly entertaining nights out.

It has been an eye-opening, mind-expanding, heart-lifting, occasionally hair-raising trip, but now I am just looking forward to getting home. A message has just been pushed under my door. It is a rather touching fax from a certain lovely lady 17,000 miles away, on the other side of the world. It simply says 'D.J. – come home'.

INDEX